# AWAY WITH WORDS

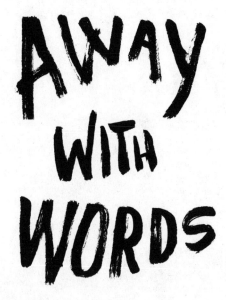

# AWAY WITH WORDS

### AN IRREVERENT TOUR THROUGH THE WORLD OF PUN COMPETITIONS

## JOE BERKOWITZ

HARPER ● PERENNIAL

NEW YORK ● LONDON ● TORONTO ● SYDNEY ● NEW DELHI ● AUCKLAND

HarperCollins books may be purchased for educational, business, or sales promotional use. For information, please email the Special Markets Department at SPsales@harpercollins.com.

FIRST EDITION

*Designed by Diahann Sturge*

Library of Congress Cataloging-in-Publication Data has been applied for.

ISBN 978-0-06-249560-0

17  18  19  20  21    LSC    10  9  8  7  6  5  4  3  2  1

*For Gabi, without whom my life would have less meaning than a bad pun.*

"Some people have a way with words, and other people . . . oh, uh, not have way."

—STEVE MARTIN

"Puns are the droppings of soaring wits."

—VICTOR HUGO

# CONTENTS

# Semifinals

# Finals

# Warm-Up

# A BRIEF GLOSSARY OF PUNS

Language has no patience. Yesterday's *That's So Raven* will become tomorrow's *Raven AF*, whether we're prepared for it or not. Although this evolution tends to happen gradually over time, some people don't have that kind of time. These brave pioneers make up their own words, either to communicate new ideas or to keep from being boring. Way more of these new words are actually puns than most people would care to admit.

The word *pun* is a blanket term, though, spanning across all different flavors of wordplay. Here's a brief glossary of the kinds you'll be seeing in this book.

- Homophonic pun: words that sound the same but have different meanings ("Walking in light rain is a *mist* opportunity")

- Homographic pun: words that are spelled the same but sound different ("Of the two types of anesthesia on offer, I'd prefer the *number* won")

- Homonymic pun: words that are spelled and sound the same ("I felt unsettled inside so I had an *evening out*")

- Portmanteau: words that combine two other words in either sound or meaning (*Lossary*, as in a glossary that is kind of a waste of time)

# INTRODUCTION

People are screaming. Throaty howls, guttural bellows, and those *whoo's* where the first two letters drop off like rocket boosters so the rest of the word can soar. I'm screaming, too. On either side of me are people I could swear I've seen on the street holding clipboards, encouraging me to switch to green renewable energy. Ordinarily, I'd cross a busy intersection to avoid those people, but right now we're on the same team, and our combined energy is making the floor thrum beneath our feet. For some reason, the couple just ahead can only muster a paltry golf clap, but they're a lonely minority, within the greater lonely minority of people who would come to an event like this.

The man standing on the lip of the stage at the Highline Ballroom in New York City looks like a magician. His hair is a wavy brown head-cape, his face is gaunt but telegenic, and he's tall enough to dangle things just out of most people's reach. Every time he says something—*alakazam!*—the room explodes.

There is nothing I've ever been surer of than the fact that this is, hands down, the best reaction to a pun I've ever seen—and I've been to Jewish summer camp in Florida. Twice.

Applauding because someone made a pun seems like a

paradox. Every lesson the world has taught me about comedy, irony, and how adults behave in public suggests that this should not be happening, that we're perhaps laughdrunk from some airborne elixir or that the delicate fabric of civilization is unraveling. But it's not.

Instead, the five hundred people in the crowd get their wish: Jargon Slayer advances to the next round of Punderdome.

IMAGINE THE BIGGEST You Had to Be There moment that has ever happened. The sky cracks open and a fleet of aliens touches down to teach Earthlings how to move solid matter with their minds. It's awesome. However, you are seriously under the weather that day and can't leave the house. Also, the aliens unlock everyone's mind powers only for one day, and only on condition that they—the aliens—not be captured on video. Never again are they seen or heard from, and telekinesis resumes not being a thing. It's hard for some people to accept that it even happened. But it did. You just had to be there.

Well, reader, I was there. Not with aliens, of course, but I have experienced something equally implausible. I spent a year attending, participating in, and documenting pun competitions, along with other activities that secretly resemble pun competitions. In that time, I received and recited more puns than even the most ardent Gene Shalit admirer would be able to endure. The book you are about to read presents these puns as they happened, and I must stress right up front that the reactions to them are not embellished.

You are going to read some puns that sound just tremendously unfunny, puns that don't make sense, puns that will get your blood boiling. This book is going to be heaved across somebody's living room, borne on a flight of rage, and it's going to scuff a banister. The important thing to know, though, is that when these puns were performed, they got the exact-size laughs and cheers described here. It strains credibility. The words *cognitive dissonance* will seem exceedingly applicable the more you read. It's going to seem as dubious as those nights in college when you left a standard issue party early and everyone told you the next day how legendary a rager it became the minute you left. But it really happened. Every gnarled, misshapen, double-meaning word is true.

You just had to be there.

# First Round

# 1

## IF THERE'S A PUN IN THE FIRST ACT

When I was seventeen, Jill O'Doyle asked if I'd seen *Titanic* yet. It was the beginning of third-period calculus, the movie had just opened, and I had some opinions about its star.

"*Titanic*?" I said, my lips curling into the fat-kid equivalent of a Billy Idol snarl. "You mean with Leonardo *DiCraprio*?"

Jill looked about a thousand detentions exhausted by this response, but to her credit, she ignored what I'd said and became suddenly fascinated by the contents of her Trapper Keeper. Our chat was over. Two weeks later, I saw *Titanic* and I cried.

As far as I can remember, this was my introduction to how puns generally go over out in the world.

Back at home, though, things were different. My dad had always been fond of pejorative twists on celebrity names. He would say "John *Revolta*" a lot, especially in the latter years of the *Look Who's Talking* franchise, but no famous person was safe. Politicians, basketball players, lead singers of bands I'd never heard of—they were all fair game. So I had come by the instinct honestly. I would leave it honestly, too.

The Leonardo DiCraprio incident was more of a failure to read the room than an indictment of puns. It was still typical, though, of what happens when a lazy wordburp rips through casual conversation. There just isn't all that much you can say to a pun—even when it's not arbitrarily bashing the dreamiest movie star on the planet. The best reactions I got in the years to come were nods, groans, and other minor acknowledgments that wordplay had just occurred. More often what I'd get were bone-chilling silences, third-degree stink eye, and heavy Twitter unfollowings. So I caved in and absorbed what I thought was the conventional wisdom: that puns are comedy kryptonite.

Until I set foot in my first pun competition, I had no idea just how many people disregard the conventional wisdom. In Brooklyn alone, it's at least four hundred a month.

Punderdome began as an ephemeral whim in the spring of 2011, when a spritely spark plug named Jo Firestone heard about one of the weirder annual traditions of Austin, Texas: the O. Henry Pun-Off World Championships. She was shocked and delighted to find out such a thing existed. Although not much of a punster herself, the rising comedian wanted to see what kind of puns Brooklyn would generate, if given not just an excuse or permission but a mandate to make them in front of an audience. Without looking any further into the O. Henry than its central premise, she booked a venue in Park Slope to stage her own version.

Considering that punning is widely thought of as the essence of the dad joke—narrowly edging out the "I'm hungry"/"Hi, hungry, I'm Dad" construction by a nose hair—it's almost poetic that Punderdome was cofounded by a comedian's dad. Fred Firestone is a retired attorney turned consultant, known for busting out frequent passable impressions of Rodney Dangerfield. When he got the call from Jo, asking for his thoughts on what a pun competition should entail, Fred offered so many suggestions that Jo ended up asking if he might want to just fly in from St. Louis to be her cohost. He said he needed more time to think about it. Then he called back ten minutes later, having already booked a plane ticket.

Around thirty of Jo's friends showed up to the first-ever Punderdome, along with some random bar hoppers she managed to pull in off the street. It was a long, gleefully disorganized night, a gloppy hellbroth of infinite gibberish. Eventually, a woman named Atilla the Pun won with a rhyming couplet about Disney Movies that culminated in *One Hundred and Pun Dalmatians*. It wasn't exactly an Ali-Frazier knockout punch. The crowd left happy enough, though, to ensure that Jo would invite them back the following month.

Over the course of sixty shows and counting, Punderdome has since evolved into a pop culture powerhouse. It's spawned two TV pilots and a licensed card game. *GQ* magazine called it one of the Funniest Nights in America in 2015. It's also developed a thriving community of champions who have dedicated fans and—believe it or not—groupies. If you live in New York and happen to make a pun in front of three or more people, one of them *will* ask if you've ever been to Punderdome.

The show's popularity is at least partly due to its prescient tapping of an underserved market. Punderdome, like the O. Henry before it, creates a right place and right time for something a lot of people feel they're not supposed to like and ought not to do. It's a bathhouse for closeted punsters, safe haven for that person in every office and classroom turning blue in the face from suppressing wordplay all day.

But that person definitely wasn't me. I was doing just fine, thank you, in terms of pun intake and distribution. When I first heard about pun competitions, there was no ministerial calling from either deep within or high above. I had no ambitions of devoting my life to coming up with words that sound like other words while in front of a crowd. In fact, at the time, I could barely think in front of a crowd at all.

ONE DAY IN June of 2015, I got an irresistible invitation. The organizers of Just for Laughs, the world's largest comedy festival, asked me to come to Montreal and moderate a panel with the creators and cast of HBO's *Silicon Valley*. It was a chance to share a stage with Mike Judge, the man behind *Beavis and Butthead* and *Office Space,* alongside a crew of comedians who were shaping up to be all-timers. Just days before, they had stuck the landing on an already-great sophomore season with a killer mic drop of a finale. Now, for their efforts, everyone involved would have to discuss the show with me in a hotel ballroom in Canada.

I accepted the offer immediately and began Yelping Montreal restaurants in search of vegetarian poutine.

As the festival drew near, though, my excitement curdled into concentrated fear-sweat. What if I froze up? What if I melted down? What if I blanked out and became a stammery, tongue-tied cumulus cloud of discomfort? My solution was overpreparation. Curate a stockpile of questions. Put them in an order that makes sense. Debate every detail, including whether to ask the audience to "give it up" for the panel, even though I'd always thought it was a weird thing to say.

By the morning of the event, fear-sweat had given way to terror-barf. I was second-guessing every question and also every piece of my wardrobe. (Fitted blue button-down, black blazer, gray Levi's. *Wait! The blazer is too warm. It has to go!*) Backstage was a *Last Supper* tableau of comedic celebrity minutia. Zach Woods and Martin Starr were being interviewed in tandem; Mike Judge hovered near a craft services table heavy on melon and brie; T.J. Miller and Thomas Middleditch were hunched over their phones, synchronized tweeting. I said hi to everybody, complimenting them on their performances in a live read of *The Big Lebowski* the previous night. Then I made a beeline for the bathroom to hide in sweet solitude.

One of the last things I'd prepared was a joke to jump-start the panel. The main characters on the show were all gawky computer geniuses, save for Erlich Bachman, who was cocky as hell and never stopped talking. The guy who played him, T.J. Miller, was a swaggering comedian and movie star, a thermonuclear thunderclap of verbosity. The contrast between him and some of the more reserved members of the panel seemed worth noting.

My opening gambit: "All right, look at this murderers' row up here. It's like the Avengers of soft-spoken comedy . . . and also T.J. Miller."

The thousand or so people in the crowd laughed. My joke worked! I chuckled into the microphone, giddy with relief, ready to dive into the first question. And that's when it started.

"You don't want . . . to do that, man," T.J. said. "I'll hit you back so hard, you'll look less like a substitute teacher than ever."

Shit. He was right. Not only about the devastating but accurate way he'd assessed my look, but also how ill-equipped I was to get into a burn contest with T.J. Miller. Chalk it up to inexperience or sheer stupidity, but somehow, when I'd thought of that joke, it never entered my mind that calling out a motor-

mouthed comedian for being just that, while onstage in front of
hundreds of his fans, after he'd been warming up for days at the
world's largest comedy festival—it hadn't dawned on me there
might be any blowback from doing that. When I'd mapped out
the panel like a Dungeons & Dragons campaign, it went: "witty
opening joke," pause for applause, and dive into first question
with three potential subquestions ready. I'd pre-bonsai'd the
decision tree. It was an epic miscalculation, though. Everyone
on the panel and in the audience was now cracking up at T.J. for
roasting me. And the floodgates were wide open.

"I had that coming," I admitted, trying to move on.

People on the show are constantly telling the main characters cautionary tales about working in Silicon Valley, so I asked
the panel if anyone had a similar experience getting started in
comedy.

T.J. Miller recited a piece of advice his costar Martin Starr
once gave him. He made it a point to mention that Martin
would have said it in more of a monotone, though. "Whereas
I'm the loud one, Joe!" he yelled and started cackling like a
supervillain. Then he looked me up and down and shook his
head. "A blue button-down and no tie."

I knew I should have kept the blazer on. No way it would've
made me sweat more than I was sweating now.

"You kinda *almost* dressed up to moderate," T.J. added.

I closed my eyes, forced a smile, and nodded, perfectly help-
less in a mess of my own making. I couldn't keep up. I couldn't
even get in the game. T.J. was wearing an outfit that was objectively ludicrous—a camo jacket over a T-shirt with an anime
wrestler's face covering the entire torso, and a teal polo collar
poking out from beneath—and I had nothing to say because
surely it could get even worse than this.

At one point, I steered into the skid to address T.J. directly. I'd read that every actor onstage had tried out for his role, so I asked why he'd ultimately been the right one for it. T.J. recited a long list of traits he shared with his counterpart, Erlich, one of which was a propensity for smoking pot all the time.

"I was so high when I came out here," he said, "I thought k.d. lang was moderating."

The audience went into hysterics as I reassessed my haircut, collar pointiness, and whatever else about me suggested the singer/songwriter behind "Constant Craving." If there was a funny or even just slightly face-saving way to respond, I couldn't find it. I'd lost my oral compass.

"I have no comeback for that," I said. It went without saying.

It wasn't just that I looked like if k.d. lang was a substitute teacher, which indeed I did, it felt like I'd become that. As the panel went further off the rails—and produced a running joke about me being in ISIS—I tried in vain to rein it in.

"Your segues are the best part of this panel," T.J. said after I tried to bring the topic back to his TV show.

It wasn't just him, though; by now, everyone was pitching in. I had fed a squad of world-class improvisers a big juicy prompt—that the moderator was fair game—and they ran wild with it. When I asked Mike Judge about what to expect in the third season of *Silicon Valley,* he simply said, "ISIS."

"You have an impossible job," Thomas Middleditch noted.

Mercifully, a P.A. signaled me with a cutoff motion and I said, "I'm getting word that ISIS is going to chop my head off if we don't stop."

Then I implored the audience to give it up for the panel.

Although the organizers of Just for Laughs assured me the event had been among the best of the festival, it was a Pyrrhic victory. The whole thing had devolved into a competition to say the funniest thing about a category—and instead of being in on it, I *was* the category.

I WENT TO Punderdome for the first time, a few months after the *Silicon Valley* incident, for the same reason I go to most inconvenient comedy events: a begrudging sense of obligation. My friend Tim Donnelly, a features writer for the *New York Post* at the time, invited me to watch him compete. I responded with the same question everybody would later ask me when I mentioned pun competitions: "What's a pun competition?"

"Well," Tim said between bites of báhn mì. "A bunch of us go onstage, we're given a topic, and then we see who can come up with the best puns on it in ninety seconds."

"What kind of puns?" I asked. Tim gave me a look of slight exasperation that I would come to know very well. It's the same face comedians make when they're introduced by occupation at a party and someone asks them to tell a joke.

"Like, um," he said, looking up at the ceiling for a second before meeting my eyes again and hoisting his sandwich. "I hope they don't *báhn mì* from the pun competition for not thinking of a better pun right now."

Fair enough. The whole thing sounded suspiciously like spoken-word fight club, but I agreed to go root Tim on. I wanted to know how any pun could be empirically better than any other pun, and who aside from the beloved science teacher at my junior high who screened *Spaceballs* twice in one school year could possibly thrive at it. My interest spiked, though, when Tim urged me to buy a ticket soon, as the show would definitely sell out. To whom?

That night's Punderdome was a special one, nine months in the making. Some of the regular champions were facing off against *New York Post* editors, the people responsible for headlines such as CLOAK AND SHAG HER (General Petraeus sex scandal) and OBAMA BEATS WEINER (Congressman Weiner sex scandal, or one of them anyway). Pun headlines are these editors' bread and butter, but it usually takes more than a few seconds to conjure and polish them into gems. Tonight, that luxury would not exist.

When I arrive at the Highline Ballroom, where I vaguely remember once seeing Gnarls Barkley, the typical bouncer pat-down feels unnecessary. The only contraband I imagine getting smuggled in are sharply waxed mustache points and extremely hot takes on the last season of *Game of Thrones*.

Inside, dozens of radically pale New Yorkers are sprawled out in each direction. Every other face has glasses perched on its nose and is talking animatedly over one of those upbeat songs by The Cure. I don't know where to stand without being in somebody's way, so I find a cozy wall space to lean against. A couple who looks like different eras of Rachel Maddow turns and asks if it's my first Punderdome. Before I can respond, roving blue lights and bass-heavy gym-techno start the show.

Looking back, I don't know exactly what I expected. Judging by Tim's impromptu báhn mì pun, the potential for excruciating sub-Schwarzenegger one-liners lurked like an Eastern European villain in the shadows. If I was at all pessimistic, though, I was the only one around for miles on that wavelength. There was an aura of effusive excitement because, I realized, I was somewhere nobody would dare go ironically. While a substantial chunk of Earth's population did all they could to insulate themselves against puns, here was an industrial-size ballroom full of people gleefully hurtling toward them. Anyone who didn't want to be here had simply *báhn'd* themselves.

Jo and Fred Firestone make their way toward the center of the stage at different speeds. Fred bounds out, beaming and pointing at people in the crowd, while Jo slinks across with a far more reserved smile, nodding a lot, as if to confirm inevitable news. Fred is a squat man in his early sixties whose balding hair is thick on the sides like a friar, giving his head a bulb shape. Jo is diminutive with an auburn-tinted crown of curls. She has a thin, reedy voice that sounds like a fairy tale.

"I'm Fred Firestone," says Fred, "And this is my *alleged* daughter, Jo."

"I'm definitely his daughter," she says and turns toward Fred. "You know I'm your daughter. My mom is your wife."

"Speaking of wives," Fred says, and then his voice gets gruff and sputtery in the way of a Rodney Dangerfield impression that would certainly embarrass offspring. "See, I tell ya, my wife, she likes to make love in the backseat of the car. Yeah, and she likes me to *drive*."

"Don't tell them that!"

A giant screen hangs above the Firestones, bedecked with a loosely R. Crumb–style illustration of the pair riding a massive Rodney Dangerfield head. Rodney is a fitting avatar for this event, I realize. He don't get no respect, and neither do puns.

"What should you never say on a plane when you see your friend Jack?" Fred asks, warming up the crowd. Several scattered voices yell, "Hijack!" Fred throws fun-size PayDay bars into the masses, a payday for giving the right answer. A silver-haired guy in a sleeveless Dead Kennedys shirt smiles at every joke that follows. The crowd is sufficiently warm.

Fred calls out the first round of puntestants and six people head toward the stage. As everyone gets situated, Jo hands each a small whiteboard and a marker. Then she announces the topic is Fine Arts. For the next ninety seconds, everyone scribbles furiously. While they do, a guy wearing a vintage Batman T-shirt and a chopstick in his man-bun leads the crowd in a sing-along to the *Friends* theme song. Tim is up first, only here he goes by Forest Wittyker, one of the first and most random pun names I hear. Because he is a regular at Punderdome, Tim will be competing against his own editors at the *New York Post* in the later rounds—if he makes it that far.

"I came up with a lot of fine arts puns," he says, "but I don't know how to frame them."

If I had an hour to meditate on a series of puns for this topic, which would obviously be my preference, I'd never come up with a more appropriate opener. Tim had ninety seconds.

The rest of his puns are arranged into a story involving some guy who was a real "MFA-*hole*," but I have a tough time concentrating because now I'm auditing my brain for puns about sculpture and decoupage. Several minutes go by and I think of zero worth sharing.

The way each round of Punderdome is decided is by audience applause, with the help of something called the human clap-o-meter. A volunteer—in this case, a college student wearing perhaps unintentional Rosie the Riveter cosplay—is asked to don a clapping apparatus. It's a jukebox-shaped wooden board, with a face hole carved out, that volunteers hold in front of themselves. The top half is divided into color wedges, ranked from Rotten Tomato to Punderful, and there's a spinnable arrow in the center that the volunteer points toward whichever wedge corresponds with how much the crowd loses its shit. In order to eliminate bias, the volunteer is blindfolded and the contestants are not announced by their pun names. Instead, Fred points to each in a random order, leaving the clap-o-meter to quantify anonymous applause. I do not envy her.

Forest Wittyker and a woman who goes by Homestar Punner move on to the next round, and a new group of challengers files across the stage. Among them is a duo called Daft Pun, who have fashioned tinfoil into medieval headgear like misfit knights errant. There's also an incongruously older gentleman named Groan Up, who looks like if John Waters were from Brooklyn. The category this time is Sources of Light.

A woman in a pool table green dress and thick black glasses wins the crowd over with her knowingly meek delivery. Her name is Words Nightmare, which I don't realize is a pun on "worst nightmare" until about three weeks later. She and Homestar Punner are among the rare female punners competing tonight, despite the diverse gender makeup of the audience.

"*Watts* going on?" Words Nightmare says, getting a laugh right away. She punctuates each pun with either a tilt of her head or a hand gesture, like she's the audience's tour guide through the vast contents of her mind.

"I hope I win tonight," she says. "I don't want any *constellation* prizes."

With a jolt, I realize how little actual puns matter in this pun competition. If Words Nightmare had just come out and screamed "*meatier* shower!" it might have been an insufferable experience. Instead, she had to find the words to frame her puns, and that's what hits the crowd's joy sensors. (She went with "I've started keeping sausages by my shampoo lately. I like a *meatier* shower.") Whatever this all was, it belonged in a stratospherically higher paygrade than the realm of the dad joke.

The next punster in the group calls himself A Little Kick in the Punt. He has an appealingly low-rent Coney Island kind of vibe, complete with a twirlable mustache, goatee, and stick-skinny limbs he contorts into an old-timey weight lifter's stretching pose before starting.

"I'm up here fa' strong puns, not *fa' lame* puns," he says, frankensteining the words together so smoothly it takes me a second to catch the Source of Light invoked.

"If you need a job to go on dates, which you do," he says, "being *canned'll* be a big problem. But I have a job, so who cares. I had a date with Ellie the other night, and the whole time I'm thinking, 'How can I give *Ellie D*?'"

It's the first overtly sexual thing anyone has said tonight, and there's an electric charge to the laughter. I look around and it occurs to me that some of the unattached English majors in the audience may end up going home with each other.

It's no surprise Words Nightmare is voted through, but when Kick in the Punt gets a lower score than Beef Chow Pun, the audience is outraged. I am, too. It's the most empathetic I've felt toward someone with a gross name since throwback rock band Diarrhea Planet failed to blow up.

In the final heat, the category is Shoes. A tall, rangy guy steps forth, dressed in all black. Later, I find out he's A Little Kick in the Punt's brother, even though their styles are dissimilar and they don't look alike. His name is Jargon Slayer.

"Sometimes the prizes we get for winning this are cool, and sometimes they're not," he says, gesturing toward the large cardboard Mystery Boxes on the table behind him. "Those are my thoughts, *re: box.*"

The crowd is into it. Someone yells "Oh!" in a celestial way that sounds like a Benedictine monk chant.

"All is fair in *loafer war*," he says, inciting a wave of groans that crests and somehow folds into a laugh.

Jargon Slayer keeps going with more and more shoe puns, measuring his words like they carry heavy import.

"Don't make them out of wax, don't fly too close to the sun," he says, letting the silence build. "Those are my *wing tips*."

After he's done, the audience is in ecstasies. The clap-o-meter needn't bother measuring his score—it's a definite 10. Jargon Slayer and Words Nightmare go on to defeat the *New York Post* editors, which leads to even more tinnitus-threatening applause. I would not have predicted hearing such massive, overwhelming crowd love tonight—or that so much of it would come from me. But here I am, cheering at least as much as I did to bring Gnarls Barkley back for an encore years ago. Some of these puns are legitimately clever, and some are irresistibly bad. The audience seemed just as happy laughing as they were groaning. It's a revelation. As a person whose default setting was anxiety, I could only envy these performers' ability to spontaneously craft the most reviled form of joke in front of five hundred people. This had to be the only place in the world where such a thing could happen. But it definitely was not.


THE O. HENRY PUN-OFF, the world's foremost pun competition, has been an Austin institution since 1978. It's a marathon of wordplay consisting of two main events spread across one long, linguistically fluid day. First up is Punniest of Show. Competitors perform a two-minute routine on a theme of their own choosing for hundreds of sun-beaten pun-funnelers. The other event is far more difficult. Punslingers is a breakneck thirty-two-person tournament where players go head-to-head, punning on all manner of topics, in front of two MCs and six judges. The opponents trade puns like boxing jabs, except it's the audience who feels like they're being pummeled. There's a five-second time limit for each turn, and the pair keeps going until either person runs out of puns about, say, country music. Meanwhile, the MCs can chime in like referees to disqualify nonpuns. All told, the day lasts something like seven hours. Some people fly halfway around the world to attend.

In creating Punderdome, the Firestones split the difference between the two O. Henry events, inventing a completely separate beast. It was only a few months after Punderdome began that word traveled down to Austin about it. The O. Henry organizers had seen similar scrappy competitions spring up and flame out since 1978. They had no idea whether the Brooklyn upstart would have any longevity, but lines of communication soon opened between them. Representatives from either side visited the other. As more and more Domers found out about the O. Henry, they started traveling down South to compete. Being crowned best punster in Brooklyn any given month was a nice incentive, but competing in Austin carried the possibility of becoming a literal world champion. What drove a person to pursue such a goal? Was it like the opposite of the Williams sisters, with parents organizing interventions instead of aggressively encouraging? I was determined to find out.

It's impossible to leave a pun competition without looking closer at the words that wallpaper your world. For instance, the day after Punderdome, I stared at Chipotle subway ads that read "Bon Appetaco" and "Porkadise Found" and tried to top them. ("Burritoyeah" and "Fajit's sake" were my best offerings at the time.) A switch had flipped on in my brain. I was developing RoboCop vision for pun possibilities. Every phrase was one tweak away from a double meaning. Suddenly, I was a thirty-five-year-old who guffawed when he realized that plans to commit incest could be called *Oedipal arrangements*.

Society and Leonardo DiCaprio had brainwashed me to be a self-hating pun monster, but perhaps I only hated puns in certain moments. I rolled my eyes at the ones in ads and lifestyle magazines, the ones that dressed a concept up in an ill-fitting business suit of "fun," and I sucked my teeth when somebody made a pun on whatever we were talking about five minutes ago, the context long since evaporated. But I was firmly on board with what I'd heard last night. Maybe I'd been wrong about other things as well.

Later that day, I decided to go to the next Punderdome, and probably the one after that. It was partly because I just wanted to hear more dope puns, and partly because I wanted what these performers had. Not the contents of the Mystery Box, which turned out to be a BeDazzler, but something intangible. I wanted their ability to find the right thing to say at the right time. The contestants had reminded me of all the snappy comebacks I'd never made, all the TV dialogue too sparkling to be real, the promise of being perpetually unstuck, a wellspring of spontaneity. These people were either performing at Punderdome because they were good at thinking on their feet, or they were good at thinking on their feet because they performed at Punderdome. Either way, I wanted to find out more about them and join them onstage. If they went to the O. Henry, I wanted to join them there, too. Over the next year, I discovered exactly what kind of individuals devote themselves to punning, and how they spent the rest of their time. Some turned out to be comedians, actors, and slam poets; others were software developers and ergonomic engineers. They punned out of a lifelong fascination, or obsession, or because they simply could not stop. They were more fun to hang out with than that sounds.

I also decided to investigate some other situations that are similar to pun competitions. I would explore TV's closest thing to Punderdome, *@Midnight,* where the comedy elite goes for guilt-free punning, and visit the headquarters of the punniest show on TV, *Bob's Burgers.* I'd investigate how *New York Post* headline writers come up with concise wording quickly, and what neuroscientists know about what happens in our brains as we're mangling language. I would dig deep into this world, hear stories from its inhabitants, and experience it all for myself. I would become Punter S. Thompson.

# 2

## WELCOME TO THE PUNDERDOME

Like wedding cakes, most trophies come topped with miniature depictions of the people they belong to. Think of the golf trophy with its gleaming golden swinger, midstroke, or the diving trophy whose arched bronzed merman looks to be transporting heavy furniture. The trophy for the O. Henry Pun-Off World Championships, though, comes in the shape of a horse's ass, as if to caution winners against the sin of hubris. A trophy in this shape succinctly sums up what it means to be the best at something a lot of people consider the worst.

Way more pun competitions exist than most sane civilians might presume. There's Minnesota's Pundamonium, Orlando Punslingers, the UK Pun Championships, the Almost Annual Pun-Off in Eureka, California, and several others. The O. Henry is without a doubt the Olympics of pun competitions, though, and Punderdome is their X Games. Both events also have their beloved champions who sometimes cross over to the other side. These heroes just tend to grace far fewer Wheaties boxes.

One of the first things to establish when getting into any new sport is who is its Michael Jordan. Even mildly serious competitive bowlers quickly learn about Earl Anthony, the Michael Jordan of bowling. Unfortunately, there's no Elo rating system to rank punsters like chess players and eSports all-stars. I searched online for a Guinness World Record along the lines of Most Decorated Competitive Wordsmith, to no avail. As far as Guinness is aware, pun competitions do not even exist. Considering there's a world record for Most Candles Blown Out by a Single Fart, though (five, if you're wondering), the sports trivia canon probably also has room for a competition that's been around almost forty years and has roots that run far deeper in cultural history. I applied online to establish one.

On the submission form, there's a field for nominating the record-holder. The name I gave is Benjamin Ziek. It didn't take much research to see that he was the most dominant player the competitive pun world has ever seen.

Ziek is buzz-cut and built like a cross between a circus strongman and *Sopranos* consigliere, complete with tree-trunk calves. For the past six years, he has never left the Austin competition without taking home a horse's ass or two, winning Punslingers four times, Punniest of Show twice, and Most Valuable Punster twice as well. His day job is night auditor at a Marriott in Burbank, but he also manages a team for Millennium Pro Wrestlers—and occasionally gets in the ring himself, under the name Lex Icon. (Think of him as independent wrestling's answer to Bobby "The Brain" Heenan.) Although Ziek has experience with stand-up and improv, his main area of expertise is the quick thinking and deep reservoirs of trivia that are the cornerstones of the game-show circuit. He is a game-show junkie through and through, with a side business that delivers a game-show experience like a traveling carnival midway.

Ziek has made appearances on five separate TV game shows and won thousands of dollars. In fact, he only made it to O. Henry for the first time, in 2009, after winning $4,400 the previous year on *1 vs. 100* and splurging on a plane ticket. His dream, he tells me, is to create a TV show where he travels around the country winning pun competitions, which seems like the kind of optimism that fuels third-party presidential candidacies. Ziek is a Gatling gun of puns that has only rarely jammed. He is clearly the Michael Jordan of the pun world. But just as a slew of physically gifted souls like Shaun White, the Flying Tomato, have managed to win at both the Olympics and the X Games, some verbal athletes have found glory at both the O. Henry and Punderdome. Among this small few, the Flying Tomato of pun competitions must be Jerzy Gwiazdowski. (The trick to unlocking the pronunciation of that last name is using *his house key*.)

AFTER THE *New York Post* event, I wanted to know everything about Jargon Slayer. Who exactly was this linguistic conquistador? I asked Tim, my conduit to the pun world, to connect us through Facebook, and he obliged. A couple weeks later, Jerzy and I are in the backyard of a Brooklyn bar called Crown Inn, sitting at a picnic table lit by a mason jar candle.

"I've always been a words guy," he says, brushing a Weird Al lock of sternum-length hair out of his eye. "You could say I've languished in language my whole life."

Language has served Jerzy Gwiazdowski well. The plays he's written have been produced on four continents, and as an actor, he once took over for Domhnall Gleeson as the lead in a Broadway show. When he's not teaching playwriting work-shops or working odd jobs, Jerzy plays small roles on TV shows like *Girls, Nurse Jackie,* and the various *Law & Order*s that are prerequisites for any self-respecting New York actor. Lately, though, these kinds of parts have started drying up. These days, Jerzy Gwiazdowski is best known for punning—a talent nearly impossible to make a living at.

Jerzy has earned two of the three major awards at O. Henry, and he's won Punderdome so many times he's lost count (four-teen). Like Ben Ziek, he wants to travel around the world to compete in every available pun competition, only he has no plans to pitch a show about it. Also like Ben Ziek, he only made it to his first O. Henry thanks to a sudden windfall—though Jerzy's came from a kick-ass tax refund and not a game-show victory.

After putting this found money toward a plane ticket to Austin, Jerzy promptly began to freak out. Maybe his com-petitors took puns way more seriously than he did, receiving black-ops training at some clandestine pun-dojo. Jerzy googled "NYC pun contest," fishing for any way to practice the dark art of wordplay, and discovered Punderdome, which was then in its second year. Under the name Do Pun to Others he com-peted for the first time and took second place against Tim. The following month, he came out on top. By the time he traveled down to Austin in the spring of 2012, Jerzy felt confident about his Punniest of Show monologue, a clever routine about states and capitals. Not only did Jerzy win, but the video of his perfor-mance ended up creating a rare viral moment for the O. Henry, getting upvoted onto the front page of Reddit.

"So, the time you won the O. Henry, that's online?" I ask.

"Yeah."

"And we can watch it right now, hypothetically?"

"I mean, yeah," he says, shrugging. "If you want."

I do want. Through a tiny iPhone screen, within napkin-flinging distance of a pair of chatty crust punks, I get my first glimpse of the O. Henry. It's an outdoor stage in broad daylight, populated by two older southern gents in goofy hats. The background is bisected lengthwise, with the top half resembling a deconstructed Texas flag, and the bottom half a colorful triptych the shade of Miss Piggy, Kermit, and Scooter, respectively. My eyes feel assaulted. Soon, a rail-thin Jerzy cautiously walks to the center of the stage and begins.

"Baby, you've got me in a state, and I fear that it's *contiguous*," he says. "I'*m-in-it-sorta* deep here. Why don't *you-ta*lk. I know what you're thinking: I *knew-him, sure*. But he cut me off, and now he wants to *connect-a-cut*."

Midway through the routine, he starts nimbly stacking sentences like Tetris pieces to put the state and the capital in a row. ("I know a lad can get lonely, and *Juneau a lass can* too.") It's a dazzling strategy. It kills.

The video of Jerzy's first O. Henry visit racked up over 150,000 YouTube hits, which in terms of punning is like two or three "Gangnam Style"s. Suddenly, Jerzy was fielding interview requests from curiosity blogs and Australian radio stations. In as much as one can attain celebrity status in the narrow field of pun competitions, Jerzy was a hot rookie sensation.

Over the next year, he sustained his momentum by competing at Punderdome, frequently in triumph. When he returned to Austin for his sophomore O. Henry, though, he blew it.

"I wanted a challenge," Jerzy says, hefting his hefeweizen.

What he gave himself was a suicide mission: a routine based on the books of the Old Testament, in order. Even in the notoriously bible-friendly state of Texas, there were no guarantees anybody would understand what he was saying.

The Bible is not inherently unpunnable. *Washington Post* columnist Alexandra Petri, who has also won at both O. Henry and Punderdome, snatched the crown with her bible routine that very year. But Jerzy's attempt was ambitious to a fault.

"Bible scholars want to know what our species' entrance was, but I want to know what our *genus's exit is*," he begins, with the fury of a Sermon on the Mount. "So I turned to math. When I like math, I hug an equation. When I *love it, I kiss numbers*."

Whenever Jerzy stops to catch his breath, face-melting awkward silences hang in the air. You can hear people clear their throats above the windless air. It's not pretty. As he continues, Jerzy starts chuckling nervously, to fill the void of zero crowd reaction. You can almost see the moment he decides to just power through and get this failed Hail Mary over with.

"Boy, it's hard to do a two-peat, isn't it?" O. Henry director Gary Hallock says after it's over, a touch of glee in his voice. "Not sure I find that routine . . . *wholly buyable*."

Jerzy did not attend the Pun-Off the following year.

When he did go again in 2015, with two years of Punderdome under his belt, it was a return to form. He nabbed MVP and came in second for Punslingers, losing only against Ben Ziek. The final round between the two was the longest in the event's history. For forty-eight minutes, Ziek and Jerzy went back and forth on the topic of numerical phrases such as "three's a crowd," which seems impossible. It's tough for me to imagine making puns on this topic for even just forty-eight seconds without disappearing from the stage in a panicky moonwalk.

At Punslingers, quantity trumps quality. The puns don't win points for being clever or funny; they just have to hold up as puns under the scrutiny of the judges. Whoever runs out of punnable phrases loses, and in this case, it fell to Jerzy. It wasn't the first time Ben Ziek defeated him either.

"He's my Salieri. Or I'm his Mozart. I don't know which," Jerzy says of his frequent opponent. "I'm gonna beat him next year, though. I have to."

Before Jerzy and Ziek can rematch again in Austin, though, there are pressing matters back here in Brooklyn. After winning the last three Punderdomes in a row, Jerzy is gearing up for an unprecedented fourth. Nobody has won that many consecutive months in the nearly five years of the event's history. Making matters more interesting, he'll be vying for this honor against Punky Brewster, the only Dome champion who has won as often as Jerzy. Punky hasn't competed in months but she's rumored to be due for a homecoming.

"I've gotta see that," I say.

"You're not just gonna see it, right?" Jerzy says. "Aren't you *pun*ticipating, too?"

He's right. It's time.

THE LINE AT Littlefield, home of Punderdome, is already Disney ride–length forty-five minutes before showtime. I kill time twirling a loose ivy vine that clings to the building's brick façade, actively tuning out a woman in golden zebra pants ranting about the rugrats she teaches.

After a few minutes, Fred Firestone begins surveying the crowd. Without his trademark Hawaiian shirt on, Fred doesn't seem quite in character yet. He's still bubbly and chatty, though, clutching a bunch of large gold rectangles whose resemblance to Wonka factory tickets seems intentional. He sidles up to people on line in a way that reminds me of Washington Square Park weed dealers. When he gets close, he asks whether I'm competing and I tell him I think so.

"Well, are you or aren't you?"

"I am!" I assure him. "But I don't have to, if more regulars show up and they need spots."

Fred shoots me a look like I just offered to tend bar in exchange for a place to sleep, and he says it's fine. He hands me a golden slip. Then he peers past me, and his face lights up.

"Hey, look at this guy," Fred calls out, walking over to where Jerzy has just joined the line. Jerzy seems embarrassed but maybe more like he's putting on a show of seeming embarrassed.

"Do you know who this fella is?" Fred asks the guy behind me, who looks preppy but not in the way of high school bullies—more like their sidekicks. "Let's just say you don't want to go on after him."

Preppy Guy smiles.

Jerzy and Fred know each other well. As the pioneer Punderdomer to compete at O. Henry, Jerzy's since become a diplomat for the two competitions, helping them forge a relationship.

Fred soon leaves, and Jerzy joins me in line. He's recovering from a hangover and he looks it, dark beneath the eyes and slouchy in stature. After workshopping a play, he spent last night watching a Packers game and consumed a beer for each of Aaron Rodgers's touchdown passes.

"And when I woke up this morning," he says, "the room was a perfect spiral."

There's usually a tone of expectation at the end of a pun, demanding a reaction from the recipient. Even though puns run rampant in this place, I don't quite know how to react to this first one delivered so casually in conversation. I could fake-laugh, but I would hate that and Jerzy would probably hate it, too. The polite thing to do is to volley a pun right back at him. I rack my brain for football words I can jam into the context of alcohol or being hungover. I remain racking for several seconds. *Good thing you have a gridiron stomach* drifts by like turgid wind, and I decide not to say it or anything else. Jerzy takes this opportunity to check his phone.

Once we're inside, he reminds me I have to come up with a *nom de pun* to give Jo Firestone when she takes my golden ticket. Jargon Slayer is a snazzy name. I'd love something like that. But there's barely time to come up with anything. My first thought is Punnilingus. Aside from the fact that this name seems like what Terry Richardson would pick if he were blackmailed into competing at Punderdome, I don't want the first thing I say to Jo Firestone to be "punnilingus." My next thought is Punter S. Thompson and it feels so appropriate I have to restrain my fist from involuntarily shooting up in the air like Bender at the end of *The Breakfast Club*.

"Good one!" Jo says as she hands me a giant name tag to write my new name on.

The crowd seems more relaxed here on their home turf than they did at the Highline Ballroom last month. A trio of women forms a skyline of severe bangs near the bar, laughing. One of them is wearing a romper with half-peeled bananas printed all over it. The area by the bar is partitioned off from the show room by a thick black curtain. A few eager beavers are strategically positioned right next to it, ready to pounce on the prime seats when the curtain is drawn. Only a couple people besides Jerzy and myself have donned name tags. Everybody else is here for the show. Baristas and web developers, assistant librarians and artisanal mayonnaise store employees. All of them just enjoying a night out with some artisanally crafted puns. It suddenly hits me that I'm about to be part of their entertainment—with no script, no practice, and no idea what the hell I'm doing. I feel like I just left the house for a long trip and I forgot to pack the right things or turn off the oven or get directions but I'm too far away to turn back. I try to think of anything entertaining to say, not even a pun necessarily, and nothing comes. I guess failure can be entertaining?

Soon, a tan, relaxed dude with a stubbly goatee and a widow's peak joins Jerzy and me. His name tag reads Punder Enlightening, but he introduces himself as Isaac. He's a friend of Jerzy's who also works in theater, directing several plays a year.

"Rekha's coming tonight," Isaac confirms. "First time in months, I hear. But I haven't been here in months either."

Jerzy nods slowly at this announcement, like a chef evaluating the sous chef's sauce. Rekha Shankar is Punky Brewster, Jerzy's friendly rival at Punderdome. The anticipated face-off is happening after all.

"I know I say this every time, but I'm really feeling off tonight," he says.

"Never seems to stop you," Isaac responds.

The two clink beer bottles and then Jerzy turns to me. "Isaac and I met in college. Back in my halcyon days."

Jerzy was two years ahead of Isaac at the University of North Carolina School of the Arts, where he'd established himself as the campus's own personal Dwayne "The Rock" Johnson, booking leads in every project. When Jerzy sat in on a lower-level movement class one day, Isaac was even a little starstruck. The two started seeing each other at parties, though, and soon they began to hang out, verbally jousting through games of

Monopoly, making gross puns about Community Chest and Baltic Avenue. Years later, after Jerzy started winning at Punderdome, he encouraged Isaac to come along. It wasn't long before the two friends were regularly going toe-to-toe in the final round, with Isaac sometimes coming out on top.

"What even *are* halcyon days?" Isaac asks.

"You know, the good old days," Jerzy says. "The salad days."

"If anyone actually refers to their best days as 'salad days,' though, those days probably weren't so great," I point out. Jerzy and Isaac suddenly look deep in thought.

Jerzy speaks first. "I don't know, I've heard that word *tossed* around a lot."

Isaac nods. "It's something that needs a-*dressing*."

"Don't be *radicchio*."

"You're *arugula* contender."

They parry back and forth so quickly I can't jump in, even if I had something good to add, which I don't. But I desperately want to get in on whatever this is.

"In a crowd of *thousands*, he's where their *eyes-land*," I blurt out.

Yikes. My instinct is to apologize, so I do. Jerzy and Isaac kind of shrug with their faces. A bad pun here apparently isn't the party foul it might be elsewhere. Apologizing actually throws the rhythm off more than a bad pun, so maybe *that's* the party foul. Everything is upside-down. What this revelation means, though, is that at least I probably won't hear anyone say "pardon the pun" tonight. I hate when people say that, as if the pun were a malevolent spirit who briefly puppeteered their vocal cords; as if they hadn't spoken up in the first place specifically to say that pun, just before disavowing it. People who say "pardon the pun" are slippery hucksters not to be trusted.

Once the black curtain parts, the crowd surges in to claim seats. Every last one is promptly filled, and the overflow spills out to each of the room's nooks and most of its crannies, including the concave space beneath the sound engineer booth. Many of the people lined up to cram in are left standing by the bar, a traffic jam turned parking lot.

A woman with a neat tidal wave of sandy brown hair, shaved close on one side, greets Jerzy with a hug.

"Remember me?" she asks, and Jerzy smiles stiffly, like he can't remember whether this is a friend or foe.

Her name is Ariel, which I will not forget because she's wearing an ocean blue sweater with Ariel the Little Mermaid across the torso. Ariel was apparently in town a couple months ago interviewing for a job on a political TV show, when she randomly heard about Punderdome. She competed that night, as P-Witty, and managed to make it to the second round. Ariel's back tonight, having landed the job, for her first Dome as a New York resident. After they shoot the shit for a minute, Jerzy does in fact remember her and even remembers one of her puns.

Ariel soon leaves to greet a friend, and I let Jerzy go off to "get in his zone," as he says. Looking for a place to stand, I burrow through the crowd to a spot in the corner. A conspicuous couple of Brooks Brothers bros scowl as they make room. Nearby, a woman with a caramel complexion and a red hoodie hunkers down in a squat, listening to headphones and swaying slightly. I can't decide whether this antisocial gesture means she's in the wrong place or exactly the right one.

Several INXS and ABBA songs later, the fifty-sixth monthly Punderdome is under way. As Jo and Fred Firestone warm up the crowd, my stomach continues its slow descent into new submarinal dimensions.

"So, for all intents and purposes tonight, a pun is going to be a play on words," Jo says from the stage. "Anything squarer than that, just, we can't. We've been drinking too much, so that's the main rule."

After hearing Jerzy's stories about how strict the rules are at the O. Henry, this is a relief. It doesn't seem to be a direct swipe at the Austin punsters—both sides are friendly with each other—but maybe it's a subtle nose-thumbing in their direction. This is, defiantly, a no-holds-barred pun competition. In fact, the whole operation feels vaguely like a wrestling league, with the beloved champions and the goofy fake names. Fred and Jo Firestone are like the Vince and Stephanie McMahon of the pun circuit. Well, maybe if the WWF had been Stephanie's idea and Vince had fewer shady political ties.

When the preamble ends and Jo reads off the names for the first round, mine is not among them. Jargon Slayer and Punder Enlightening are, though.

"Are you guys ready to do the Dome?" Fred asks the crowd as the puntestants walk onstage.

The first category tonight is School Supplies. All six competitors start scrawling on their boards as a guy in leather pants sings the *Fresh Prince of Bel-Air* theme song. Everybody sings along, and it sounds like recess at a hipster elementary school.

Isaac is up first, and he unfurls a flurry of puns in a staccato rhythm, one after the other, rat-a-tat-tat. His set concludes with a big winner: "My favorite rappers? I have 88 of them. *TI? 89.*"

It's not often you see adults go legit apeshit over a hybrid hip-hop/calculator pun.

If Looks Could Kale is on next. I recognize him from before the show started, when he approached Jerzy by the bar and whispered in his ear conspiratorially. The reason I remember

him is that he's wearing a Hawaiian shirt like the kind the Firestones wear, which seems not by accident.

"It's Back to School season," he starts. "Did, uh, anyone
have a hard time getting here today with all these kids walking
around . . . with their *bratpacks*?"

Oof. The crowd groans in a way I haven't heard yet in my
limited pun experience, with a kind of aggrieved inflection na-
tive to sports bars during a big turnover. I've been wondering
since my Thousand Island pun earlier tonight about the distinction between good puns and bad puns. Is there a Green-
wich Mean Time of wordplay, some definitive standard to steer
by? Or do you just know Bad Puns when you see them, like that
horny Supreme Court justice said he knew pornography? In
any case, I know it instinctively, in my bones, that "bratpacks"
is a Bad Pun. This will be the first kind of Bad Pun I categorize
on this journey: the False Alert. It's when a word combination
is either too simple, familiar, or obvious to be worth mentioning, but then you still do it anyway. Your heart was in the right
place—you saw something and said something—it just turned
out to be absolutely nothing at all.

(Some people argue that all puns are this kind of pun.)

A pity laugh rings out from somewhere at "bratpacks," but
it only draws attention to the absence of any other laughs. Hard
to imagine there's any coming back from a start like this, and
there isn't. When Kale finishes, he takes a bow and salutes.

"We're bringing up a multitime Dome champion now," Fred
says after the applause dims. "He's going for a record four in a
row. Please welcome: Jargon Slayerrrr!"

Fred airs the name out like a wrestling announcer while
Jerzy ambles over to the microphone, looking composed.

"I'm glad they're reviving Farm Aid, because I'm *pro-tractor*," he says, getting a laugh.

"Instead of going school-supply shopping, I went to a football game. But I don't really like watching football in October . . . to me, it's more of a *Jan*Sport."

The crowd is eating up every word, just like they did at the previous show. One of the blue-shirted finance dudes nearby even nudges another in the arm, which is as close as they've come so far to anything like an emotional response. The more specific Jerzy gets, the more applause he gets in return. Note to self: bring on the obscure brand names!

"I'll leave you with this," Jerzy eventually says, like comedians do when teeing up their closers. "You know, I see a lot of men in the audience with big bushy beards and I'm assuming you're all wild game hunters, but if you find out a deer you're hunting is a doe, please don't *trap or keep her*."

The clapping intensifies as Jerzy nods and falls back in line. When the clap-o-meter is brought forth, the crowd chooses him, Isaac, and a guy named Pun Tzu: The Art of Word.

Jo and Fred immediately summon a fresh batch of players, and Punter S. Thompson again is not among them. I let out a long, jagged breath and try to psych myself up. *If there's any trouble, just remember: words that sound like other words.*

When my name finally is called, I slither through the crowd in a daze and float onto the stage. Jo shoves a small, lined whiteboard and a marker into my hands. Meanwhile, Fred introduces a woman with searing bright red hair, like magma coating her head, to sing while we write down our puns. This is it.

Jo announces the category: Medicine. I'm relieved at first.

Such a broad topic! Then I'm outraged when puns fail to magically appear in my brain. The redhead starts singing the *Duck-Tales* theme song and I try to make puns. My frenzied mental Rolodex scroll goes like this: "medicine," "sickness," "doctor." Doctor? That sounds like *docked her.* That's . . . something. What's next? "Injection." What's funny or interesting about "injection"? Nothing. Let's move on. How about "polio"? I can turn that into *poly, yo.* But what does that even mean? Maybe "roly *poly, yo*"? Jesus, time is almost up already. And all I can think about is the goddamn *DuckTales* theme song. Really, *DuckTales* ducks? You "might solve a mystery or rewrite history"? You're not rewriting jackshit.

In a panic, I start writing down any medical-themed words I can think of. Maybe the puns will materialize once I see them on the board! They don't. Time is up, and Jo asks for our markers. I hand mine over. It doesn't seem possible that I've only jotted down a handful of pun ideas and one of them is just the word *cast.* What's wrong with me? Maybe I do need a doctor.

As the first puntestant, Verbal Kint, timidly recites his puns, my mind is racing desperately. No matter how much I look down at the words on the board, they don't resolve themselves into coherency, or even the special incoherency that is the coin of the realm here. Where do I start? What do I say? One other pun occurs to me, but before I decide how I'm going to say it or any of my other puns, Fred is calling out Punter S. Thompson and looking at me. Time is up.

I walk over to the mic and force myself to look out into the crowd. Even though there are hundreds of people watching, waiting for me to say something, it doesn't look like it. The lights are so bright I can't really make out much beyond the first row. Shadowy, faceless figures loom like something from a nightmare, except the haziness is comforting since it seems to represent fewer people.

"This is going to be . . . so quick, you guys," I say, and the crowd laughs. Praise Yahweh!

"I kind of *lipo-suck* at puns."

This was the one I thought of while staring at my board, and it gets another laugh. The audience suddenly feels less like an enemy.

"I had to get that surgery because I was too roly *poly, yo*."

This time, the laugh is even bigger. I'm on a roll!

"But the surgeon kind of messed up, so they *docked her* pay."

The audience groan-laughs, but it's a laugh nonetheless. What I have said is pretty much a False Alert pun of the highest order, but since it sort of fit what could loosely be called the "narrative" I was spinning, the crowd gave me a pass.

"All right, you do not want to hear what else I have written down," I say and walk back. Jerzy gives me a thumbs-up from the side of the stage. The nervous energy drains from my body all at once, like piñata candy. *That could've gone much worse!*

I'd been so caught up in a dread spiral that I hadn't realized the woman with headphones nearby earlier was standing next to me onstage now. When Fred calls out Punky Brewster, she moves forward, some strut in her step.

"I went to vet school, you guys, so I know every type of goose noise," she says. "Guess you could say I'm a *honkologist*."

The crowd roars. While I struggled to clear thirty seconds onstage, Rekha makes two minutes feel like all the time in the world. The puns keep coming until she finally concludes with this knuckleball: "I have a high-definition TV and I eat, sleep, and breathe it. I basically *pee HD*."

Rekha's time away had no effect on her punning ability.

Next up is a goofy guy-girl duo named Punderella, who end their set by providing their actual phone numbers, then it's the preppy guy who was in line behind me, a first-timer going by James Pun der Speak. He has as few puns as I did, but he sets each one up with these incredibly convoluted stories that gradually win the crowd over.

"This girl from my hometown, which was near a chemical factory, her name was Anna, and she used to run around a lot," he says, smiling like a little kid about to say a swear. "So, after a while, her T-shirt would get stinky from all the methane in the air, and to knock you out the doctors gave you *Anna's T-shirt*."

The laugh he gets is a groan-laugh. But it's a really big groan-laugh.

At the end of the round, when the human clap-o-meter emerges, we each have a moment to appeal to the crowd for applause. Funky dance moves are allowed, as are actual begging and pretty much anything else short of bribery—although one elfin boy does jokingly throw a few dollars in the air. Then the clap-o-meter reveals our fate.

Verbal Kint slinks out to face the crowd first and doesn't get much response. The clap-o-meter calls it a 6. Low energy does not seem to be the way to go. When it's my turn, I haul ass to the edge of the stage with a mock-surprised smile, like I just realized the audience is there, and do a silly mechanical hand wave. People whoop and holler. I get a 7. It's not enough to advance to the next round, but at least someone else did worse.

"You were awesome," Jerzy tells me when I get offstage. I can't take a compliment anyway, but this feels more than usual like someone blowing sunshine up my ass.

"I only had, like, three or four puns," I protest. (It was definitely three.)

"They were all good, though! It's quality, not quantity."

This is the exact opposite of how Jerzy described O. Henry.

"My mouth was watering from your category," Jerzy adds. "I mean, Viagra alone."

How could I have forgotten Viagra! So many puns left on the table. Now that Jerzy mentioned it, Medicine truly was a rich category. So many long, syllabically outlandish words. So many different types of doctors, injuries, bones, diseases, equipment. Hodgkin's lymphoma! I had squandered my turn. Now I'm left with a sharp feeling of loss unlike any other, which I decide to call Punner's Remorse.

A few minutes later, the second round begins. Fred calls out for Jerzy with the first batch of players. The category is: Underwear. When it's his turn, Jerzy starts off with some stage banter.

"Fred: I'm assuming briefs. And *Jo: boxers*?" Jo makes a face like *fine, why not* and there are muted cheers from the crowd, who either do not recall the affordably priced '90s men's underwear brand, Joe Boxer, or do not care.

"I'll keep this *brief*," Jerzy says. "I eschew shirts and I *pan tees*."

The audience thaws, but only a little.

"Come on, this is my best routine, this is my *core set*."

As some solid cheers roll in, he adds, "*Spanx*," and the cheers get louder.

"I just play it where it *lace*. That's how I pun. It's my *victorious secret*."

This line gets his biggest reaction yet. Jerzy looks around at the hollering crowd and nods, leaving on a high note. Closely following him is James Pun der Speak, the guy with the long, drawn-out setups. He packs in just as much deliriously dorky exposition as before. By the time he gets finished, the audience could not be more on his side. I search Jerzy's face onstage and it's unclear whether he's worried. But he probably should be.

Isaac begins like Jerzy did—by bringing Fred into the mix. "Were you in California recently, Fred? I can tell by the odor, because *Fred reeks of Hollywood*." The crowd goes bananas and keeps up the energy throughout Isaac's turn.

The final participant in this round is P-Witty. She seems very excited to be up, her entire face a quivering grin. "Of *corsets* . . . hard to follow all these talented people, but I'll try and *see* it *through*," she says. This second one barely qualifies as a pun, but Ariel says it with kind of a nonthreatening Cheshire Cat smile and it lands.

"The right bra really puts me in *matin' form*," she continues. "But when it comes to making breakfast the next morning, I'm quite the *pan-tease*."

The audience goes nuts, even though they've already heard puns on panties and corsets from Jerzy—maybe even more so, because of how different the two are from each other.

After everyone finishes, James Pun der Speak leads the group with a 10 from the clap-o-meter, while Jargon Slayer, Punder Enlightening, and P-Witty all tie at 9.5. Since only two can advance to the semifinals, each of the three has one more awkward opportunity to plead for applause. Having just participated in this hammy pageantry myself, I sympathize. There's only so much galloping across the stage or pretend-lassoing the crowd you can do before you just feel dead inside. Of these last three contestants, P-Witty gets the most applause. Isaac is second. Jerzy is out. He leaves the stage straight-faced, without ever betraying that he just ended a three-month streak.

After a strong semifinal round, Rekha ends up in a climactic pun-off with Isaac. They fling puns back and forth for two minutes, words flying by ferociously, the audience working it-self into a frothy lather. When it's time for the audience to vote, Punky Brewster pulls more cheers. Punderdome is hers.

After it's all over, I catch up to Jerzy and ask whether he blames his loss on a skewed clap-o-meter. He doesn't. Instead, he blames himself. He blames himself a lot.

"I bungled my setups and meandered through that second round," he says. "I could've done a whole string of bra puns—A cup, B cup, C cup—but I got hung up on putting them together in a story. I shouldn't have even made it to that clap-off."

Jerzy shakes his head and looks at me with a crooked smile.

"I sometimes get embarrassed by how seriously I take this," he says.

The way he takes it most seriously is by holding himself to the stricter O. Henry standards, even here, where anything the audience accepts as a pun is considered a pun. It's an extra degree of difficulty most people in the crowd probably don't notice, but it's something that might give him an edge when he faces off against Ziek next spring. Did everybody in Austin share this Garry Kasparov–like intensity with Jerzy? Now that I'd experienced Punderdome firsthand, and heard about the O. Henry from a Brooklyn perspective, perhaps it was time to head down South and hear more straight from the horse's ass.

# 3

# THE PLACE BEYOND THE PUNS

The number one factoid most people know about the late author O. Henry is that he was named after a candy bar, or a candy bar was named after him. At a distant second, they might also know that many of his stories ended with proto-Shyamalanian plot twists. *The couple in* The Gift of the Magi *ruins Christmas . . . by being really terrible at Christmas.* Ironic twist endings like these were his signature. So there's a chance that O. Henry, whose real name was William Sidney Porter, is ROFLing in his grave about the twist in the story of his namesake Pun-Off. It turns out the world's leading pun competition is named after an author with an even less substantial connection to punning than he has to peanuts, chocolate, and fudge.

Nestled amid the steel-and-glass-engorged metropolitan cityscape of downtown Austin, like an apple inside a tool chest, is the taupe-colored cottage where O. Henry lived between 1893 and 1895. The house rests atop the kind of flood-proof brick stilts and crosshatched gating common to southern homes that have been uprooted and moved, which this one has. It's a charming old place. You can easily picture its former owner cooling his heels on a porch swing, drinking entire oceans of bourbon, if not for the placard in the garden with a picture of his face that reads THE O. HENRY MUSEUM.

The QR code is a bit anachronistic, too.

An underburdened tour guide named Grant lets me in through a door with a stained-glass panel like a Mondrian grid painting and starts filling me in on O. Henry history. During the twelve years he spent in Austin, Porter was a Renaissance man. He held multiple odd jobs, played mandolin in local bands, and published a satirical weekly newsletter, *The Rolling Stone*. Then in 1895, it all fell apart. His wife was diagnosed with tuberculosis just as he was indicted for embezzling from the bank that employed him. Rather than face the music, Porter split town for Houston, and stayed there well beyond his court date, as his wife's health deteriorated back home.

If Grant is paying attention, he can probably tell from my face that with every new detail I'm rapidly falling out of muted admiration for O. Henry.

As the spiel continues, we walk through the Porters' bedroom. I feel like a ghost cursed to haunt the turn-of-the-century American South. Floorboards creak with the precision of a horror movie foley, the framed photos are Civil War sepia, and a black church crown lies ominously atop the bed, as though its owner might at any moment cross dimensions and reclaim it. Through a slightly askew door I can see the back office and Grant's desktop computer and venti Starbucks cup, bringing me back to the present day and the tale of O. Henry.

After Porter's wife, Athol, died, he was convicted and sentenced to five years in prison. It was only then, locked away, that he began publishing under a pseudonym the short stories for which a nationwide annual award now bears his name. Upon earning an early release for good behavior, Porter moved to New York and signed a contract with the *New York World* to write a short story each week under the name O. Henry. Ultimately, he published 370-odd stories, although an unpublished bonus story is available at the museum. It's called "As Others See Us," and a sign adorned with a floating, Illuminatic eyeball says it can be mine for just $45. (Hard pass.)

In 1910, O. Henry died from cirrhosis at age forty-eight. Considering the author's legendary alcoholism, it would be a misnomer to call his death a twist ending. Now that we've wrapped up O. Henry's story, though, one pivotal detail is still missing.

"What's the tie-in to punning?" I ask. "Was he just really into wordplay?"

"Between you and me, he was not a huge punner," Grant says. "That connection was made between the museum and the Pun-Off early on because it was held here, and it just stuck."

My cursory investigation into the work of O. Henry had borne this idea out. Although he did name one of his stories "A Midsummer Knight's Dream," the author's work is largely pun-free. For all anyone knew, O. Henry in fact *hated* puns, but he was more likely just too busy being a garbage monster to his wife to form a concrete opinion on them. Any correlations that could be made between William Sidney Porter and pun competitions are tenuous at best. The author was under the gun with his weekly contract, so he had to force himself to be creative in a narrow window of time—a challenge he shares with Pun-Off participants. Also, a twist ending itself is a misdirection that makes its audience think one thing while the story does another. In a very loose and generous sense, that is what a pun does—even if most puns usually just sound like a minor speech impediment. The truth may simply be that O. Henry lived in a house that became a museum and whose vast public backyard eventually attracted a pun competition. It's a perfectly fine explanation for why the event came to be named after the author. A bit of a reach, maybe, but what is punning if not a series of exceptional reaches? How the Pun-Off ended up existing in the first place is a whole other story.

PUN COMPETITIONS SEEM like something that could only exist in the frivolous present, or like some weird bullshit I made up. But according to John Pollack, who wrote the definitive book on puns, *The Pun Also Rises,* they actually go way back.

"This is something that crosses all major languages and cultures in history," Pollack says over the phone.

Apparently, wherever you are in the world, just about, a precedent exists of people trying to top each other with wordplay for various reasons. There's an ages-old tradition among Chamulan men near San Juan, in which they hold verbal duels called k'ehel k'op, often involving puns. (The example Pollack offers is convoluted and loses something in translation, but it definitely hinges on an insult about scrotums.) Pun-filled poetry duels have also been a fixture at Palestinian weddings for centuries. In the United States, pun competitions have even found their way into politics from time to time. An 1850 debate over slavery between Senators Lewis Cass and Horace Mann, for instance, turned into a bizarre ad hominem pun-off, one that seems highly inappropriate in retrospect, given what was at stake. The O. Henry is the longest-running official pun competition in history, though, in addition to being the most prestigious and the most rigorous.

There are conflicting stories about how the event was born. Some say its roots are inextricably tied to Austin's annual block party, the Pecan Street Festival, which began in 1978—the same year as the first recorded O. Henry. The apocryphal tale is that during the festival, a crowd organically gathered in the open space behind the museum known as Brush Square, and an informal pun cipher broke out. The impromptu event was so much fun that everyone agreed to do it again the following year, and thus a tradition shrugged into existence. A lot of people make puns by accident; of *course* they might also make a pun competition by accident.

Except maybe they didn't. Gary Hallock, the director of the O. Henry for the past twenty-five years, has his doubts. Digging through the archives recently, he came across fliers for the first-ever Pun-Off. Their mere existence casts doubt on any account of the event originating spontaneously. The fliers ask interested parties to submit puns and limericks in writing for a contest, and to attend an award ceremony at the museum. (If you think the Oscars can get tedious, imagine a limerick contest acceptance speech.) Somehow this almost oppressively boring-sounding event evolved into a pun-off.

Although Gary is unsure which version of the origin story is absolutely true, those earliest days are the only ones he can't discuss with eyewitness authority. Gary became a competitor in the mid-'80s, before retiring to join the organizing committee in 1990. Now, he is the unquestioned capo di tutti capi of the O. Henry Pun-Off, with a stronger connection to it than anyone else alive. He's the reason I have come to Austin.

ALTHOUGH IT'S BECOME passé by now, one longtime mantra of this city is Keep Austin Weird. It's splashed across T-shirts sold at Zilker Park during the annual Kite Festival, it's plastered on paint-peeled bumpers of Toyota Tercels en route to yarn-bomb a tree, probably, and it's nowhere near the nude bodies undulating in the clothing-optional swimming park called Hippie Hollow. Although the vast empire of high-rises and high-end restaurants have added a slick sheen recently, Austin is still indeed weird. Its weirdness is thrust upon you the moment you arrive at the airport, greeted by fifteen-foot, psychedelically colored guitars in a V-formation around the baggage claim, as if standing sentry lest ill-tempered mutant drums invade. If the town in *Footloose* was weird for outlawing dancing, Austin seems like the type of weird where dancing might be enforced on certain government holidays. It's a weirdness that encompasses Brooklyn's, in that both places seem like they might have a hopscotch league, but Austin's stands out more for being an oasis in the reddest of red states. The friends I'm staying with live next to a chrome rocket of a food trailer called Ms P's Electric Cock, and a wax museum that looks like a grimy gothic castle with functional dungeon. When I go for a run, it's over a bridge known colloquially as Bat Bridge, for reasons I don't want spelled out until I am far away from the bridge. This city is undeniably weird and the O. Henry Pun-Off belongs here.

Punning itself may not be that weird, but the ceaseless spigot of puns that flows unimpeded at the Pun-Off might as well be directed by David Cronenberg. To oblivious passersby, it must sound like a foreign language one intuitively knows to be Elvish or Klingon, a knotty thicket of nerd twaddle. To the people inside, though, it's paradise. Anywhere else, the chance of being overheard could be embarrassing, but not here. Those who are magnetically pulled to the Pun-Off are like Amish teens on Rumspringa. For one weekend, any and all interruptive, conversation-killing word balloon animals are not only welcome—they're encouraged. There is no safe word here. (If there were, though, it would be a pun and it would be *horrible*.)

For Gary Hallock, an old school Austinite, this sanctuary has no exit. Puns are an indelible part of his life, year-round. The green zone this town has created for ardent wordplay enthusiasts has encroached ever further into Hallock's head, annexing his brain and claiming it as pun country.

Beneath a rotating haberdashery of unconventional headgear, Gary has a friendly face with soft-blue eyes and deep-set laugh lines, probably collateral pun damage. His hair is the color of sidewalk, but his bushy eyebrows are a shade darker. He has a rascally gleam in his eye, like he's always either just heard a joke or is about to deliver one. As Gary tells me his life story, though, he slips in very few puns. It's unclear whether the omission is for my benefit—all the unmade puns quietly eating him up inside. Puns are there in his waking hours, and they're there when he goes to sleep.

"I put music on in the background at night to keep the idle parts of my brain from thinking about puns," Gary tells me. "I fall asleep with a little speaker in my pillow, listening to talk radio, because if I don't, I will lie awake thinking of stuff, and inevitably, I'll think of a pun, and then I'll wish I could get up and go write it down."

We're inside of a vegan ice cream shop in North Austin that Gary's friend Valerie Ward owns. You can tell one of Gary's friends owns it because we're seated perpendicular to a doctored poster for the film *A Time to Kill* that now reads *A Time to Kale*. A young Matthew McConaughey, sleek as an otter, is arguing a court case, his clenched, emotive fist made to look as if it's clutching a stalk of kale. When I gesture toward it, Gary chortles. He has probably heard or said the word *kale* in place of *kill* thousands of times more than the average human.

Gary became a punster by default. Growing up, he'd strived to be a comedian, dutifully going to open mics and doing his time onstage. It just never gelled, though. All it took was one round at the O. Henry for him to realize he was a punster who enjoyed comedy and not a comedian who enjoyed puns. Gary admires stand-up comics who can get away with puns, but he recognizes that they're few and far between. (He cites as an example Carrot Top, the shockingly jacked prop comedy golem fated to haunt Las Vegas forever like Jack Nicholson in *The Shining*.) Following that first O. Henry, Gary spent the next thirty years deeply involved in pun competitions. It's long since become an integral part of his identity. He may be a property manager by trade, but that's not who he is. He is Mr. Pun.

"When you have a reputation like I do, any time I open my mouth, people are expecting it, and bracing for it, and cringing," he says. "When I start talking, I can sense that tension. People are waiting for me to throw a pun in. So if I do go ahead and throw one in to relieve the tension, people think that's the point I was trying to make, and they miss the point. It's like dressing in a clown costume and expecting people to take you seriously. Because I'm basically in a clown costume 24/7."

Gary first competed in the Pun-Off in 1985, and did not do particularly well. He kept coming back, though, until he won first place four years later. At that point, he decided to retire, going out on top like when Michael Strahan left the Giants and also when he left *Live! With Kelly & Michael*. Gary sensed that the competition had grown a tad stale over the past few years and needed some shaking up. When he spoke to the museum curator about it, she charged him with restoring the O. Henry to its former glory the following year. Gary accepted, forming a committee of like-minded word-nerds to assist with the reformation, and founding a group called PUNY—Punsters United Nearly Yearly. Together, they codified some long unspoken rules of the competition. They also added "World Championships" to the title, so that upstarts like the Almost Annual Pun Competition in Eureka, California, wouldn't beat them to the punch.

On my flight down to Austin, I watched a documentary called *Pun-Smoke,* which chronicled the twenty-fifth annual O. Henry Pun-Off back in 2002. It cost $35 on eBay and is definitely nowhere to be found for free on YouTube or any of the less sketchy torrent sites. *Pun-Smoke* was only thirteen years old when I watched it, but it already felt like an artifact from a bygone era. The movie exists in a moment that would become the precise dividing line between what the O. Henry was in the 1980s and 1990s, and what it is now.

*Pun-Smoke* follows the rivalry between Alex "The Terminator" Ramirez, a graybeard with a fishmouth who always looks immensely satisfied with himself, and Brian Oakley, a relative newcomer in a Hawaiian shirt who seems rather laid-back until he gets started on the subject of Pun-Off strategy, which he does often. (Gary is there, too, rocking what looks to be a train conductor's cap with two tweaked Kermit eyes on top.) During one Punslingers skirmish, Ramirez and Oakley stand in front of an enormous American flag, flinging puns back and forth, sometimes in Q&A form, like a knock-knock joke tennis match. It gets intense. Even after meeting people like Jerzy, it's surprising how seriously people in the film take the competition and punning in general. One of the players drives a Mustang GT whose license plate reads "LV-2 PUN," which seems like a thing one should be legally required to put on their online dating profile. What's most striking about the movie is how different this world seems from Punderdome, where the oldest person onstage, besides Fred Firestone, is maybe thirty-five years old and also me. I'd be shocked if any of the competitors in *Pun-Smoke* had not yet had a colonoscopy.

Everything changed within a few years, though. The improv scene in Austin galvanized around 2005, and several of those performers started competing in the O. Henry Pun-Off. This infusion of fresh creative blood, bringing in talented punsters like Dav Wallace, Matt Pollock, and vegan ice cream impresario Valerie Ward, arrived just as some of the old guard featured in *Pun-Smoke,* like Brian Oakley and David Gugenheim, retired to join Gary Hallock on the organizing committee. Around the same time, YouTube revolutionized the possibilities of viewing videos. Punniest of Show routines and Punslingers showdowns soon began to circulate online. Not only did these videos spread awareness of competitive punning to people who didn't know it existed, they also served as a comprehensive how-to manual. Between the improv contingent's creativity and YouTube's instructional power, competition suddenly got a lot stiffer. What followed was an entirely new breed of turbo-punster like Ben Ziek and Jerzy Gwiazdowski.

In less than five years, Punderdome has already undergone a similar quantum leap in the skills of its top players. The people who won at the earliest Punderdomes would not stand a chance against Punky Brewster or Words Nightmare. They've since become dodo birds in the survival of the wittiest. This is the kind of evolution that happens in any competitive medium over a long enough timeline. It's the same reason the home run arms race escalated so much in late-1990s pro baseball, minus the steroids. (Pun competition steroids consist of hours spent practicing, and possibly beta-blockers.)

However, Gary doesn't think the Domers are as fully developed as the O. Henry crowd, and he's not shy about it.

About a month after my first Punderdome, a vacationing Gary finally attended the Brooklyn event himself for the first time ever. It was a raucous post-Halloween show dominated by Isaac, who narrowly beat out Jerzy and also tied for first in the costume contest—dressed as an Internet Explorer in a safari outfit covered with cookies, open Tabs (the soda), and a sign over his junk that read PRIVATE BROWSING.

Gary was not impressed.

"It was everything I feared it might be and more: alcohol, indoor venue, and loose rules, " he says, shaking his head. He didn't keep his distaste a secret that night, either.

At one point, Jo Firestone invited Gary onstage to pitch the crowd on the O. Henry. "If you like this, you'll love Austin," he said. "Except down there we demand you make *real* puns." I've heard more enticing ads for unanesthecized dental surgery.

What Gary means by "not real" is something he calls a Matt Lauer Pun. It's a withering qualifier for wordplay that involves a phrase related to the topic, but lacking the actual substitution that gives a pun its bona fides. (Why exactly Matt Lauer has been singled out is unclear, but I suspect it comes down to Gary having caught the *Today* show on a particularly rough morning.) It's something he vigilantly opposes at O. Henry.

"We catch a lot of heat for it sometimes when the contestants say something that's really funny but not a pun," Gary says. "The crowd boos and everybody groans like 'Give him a break, it was funny!' Yes, maybe it was, but it was not a pun!"

Gary punctuates his point by wagging his finger and giving me a deep *aha!* look.

"If the topic is railroads, we will not accept anything like, 'I hope we stay on track.' That's a Matt Lauer Pun."

"What about 'Keep it *rail*?' I ask, and he nods vigorously.

The other issue Gary had with his visit to Punderdome was that it wasn't dirty enough. This is surprising since O. Henry is a more family-friendly show, and in only a few trips to Punderdome I've already heard at least half of the *Kama Sutra* translated into sex puns.

"One of the categories when I was at Punderdome was The Bathroom, so right away I go to bathroom humor," Gary says. "But none of the contestants did anything risqué or bathroom humor–like. Nothing *feces*-tious. They did tile, plumbing, a bar of soap. But they could've gone a whole other way."

"A . . . *hole* other way?" I cut in, and Gary ignores me.

"They could've done much more actual bathroom humor."

"'I don't want a piece of victory, I like my *glory whole*,'" I say.

Gary stares blankly for a moment and says, "You don't have to impress me, Joe."

Just as the level of gameplay has advanced over the years, the organizers and judges have had to change the way they create and police the game itself. In the same way that *Top Chef* continually introduces tougher ingredient combinations to match the versatility of contestants who've watched years of *Top Chef*, the O. Henry organizers keep raising the bar ever skyward. Any potential new topic is as heavily vetted as Supreme Court justices (a topic that incidentally seems like one that would end up in Punslingers). In the lead-up to the Pun-Off each year, Gary meets with his fellow organizers to field-test topics and make sure they'll be challenging enough for the likes of Ziek and Jerzy. When Gary mentions that the team is still refining this year's topics, I ask if I can join in on a session. After a moment of consideration, Gary whips out a chunky cell phone and arranges a summit the following day with David Gugenheim and Brian Oakley, the new O. Henry director and the champion from *Pun-Smoke,* respectively. It's on.

"I'm just warning you, though, if you get the three of us in a room together, there'll be so many puns on puns on puns, it'll drive you nuts," Gary says, his eyes projecting grave concern. "Like, actual Looney Tunes."

It was a risk I was willing to take.

We're sitting on the rustically kitsch patio of a spot called Spider House and I feel summarily outhipped by the entire bar. In every direction, there are overtattooed, adventurously coiffed college students lounging in mismatched lawn furniture sets beneath rickety umbrellas. Meanwhile, the median age at this table is roughly fifty-three and one of us is wearing a T-shirt that reads PUNS NOT GUNS.

The last to arrive is Gary, he of the aforementioned T-shirt. He is late because he has neither texting capability nor voice mail on his phone, and he'd been waiting for one of us to call and give him directions—which of course nobody did. I recognize Brian Oakley from *Pun-Smoke,* though he looks more weathered and gray than he did in 2002. David Gugenheim looks familiar, too, although he was less of a pronounced presence in *Pun-Smoke.* Brian works as a nurse, and David is in advertising, where he tries to jam puns into the taglines of every assignment that comes across his desk. He has the kind of perfectly round head most bald men hope for, with a white Vandyke beard like closely cropped Spanish moss. Both are known as equally talented punsters, although Brian is the only one David faced off against in their day whom he never beat.

Brian has brought a leather satchel filled with this year's O. Henry Pun-Off topics, which he carries with the gravity of a henchman handcuffed to the nuclear codes. Together these papers tell the story of how this process has changed over time. The organizers used to cycle through the same fifty topics each year, but not anymore. The committee is now dedicated to continual fine-tuning, putting potential new topics through rigorous scrutiny. The team challenges itself to wring at least fifty commonly associated words out of each prospective topic before officially advancing it into rotation. Any fewer, and the topic is deemed a dud. What threatens to sink any given round of Punslingers into chaos is that an infinite supply of words could be considered 'commonly associated' with other words by the transitive property. These meetings are meant to predetermine just how far down the rabbit hole the organizers are willing to let players go. Apparently, the O. Henry is always just a hairsbreadth away from descending into a grotty swamp of nonregulation puns.

Brian rips open his satchel, at which point I see that he has fresh scars on his hand, and pulls out an older list of O. Henry topics that have passed muster. Then he begins verbally removing the veil of Maya that shrouds this mysterious process.

"So, we write 'Blades' on an index card and the first thing we do is ask: Are we gonna take all the parts of a blade? Are we gonna reward people for knowing the difference between a tang and a hilt? Yeah, we're gonna reward that. And we'll also take the names Bubba and Gerber and Old Timer."

Brian seems to know more about knives than any person I have ever met. Before I can respond in any way, he continues.

"But then, do we take all the verbs you can do with a knife—slice, dice, cut? Maybe. Then you get to cooking—paring knife, butcher knife, machete—and that's when it gets complicated."

"We won't take ma*chete*," David cuts in, pronouncing it excrementally. "This is a family-friendly event."

"Hell, I won't take ma*chete* off anybody," Brian says.

"He's not *whittling* Dixie," Gary adds, polishing the prescription glasses that hang from a cord around his neck.

I'm starting to see why Gary warned me about getting him and the other two Marx Brothers in a room together, but it is too late. I bought the ticket, and I'm taking the ride.

"Do we take razor? Yes, we do," Brian says, arms crossed on the table like an edgy sociology professor sitting backward in a chair, possibly about to use the word *sheeple*. "But if you're taking razor, you gotta take Gillette."

"And if you take *Jillette*," David says, grinning. "You gotta take Penn."

"And then you're taking *Schick* from everybody."

I look closely at the list that has blades on it, mainly so I don't have to look Brian in the face during an aggressive display of knife knowledge. Every topic on the list is placed next to the year it was last used and which round it landed in. Some of these topics represent pet projects the committee dreamed up, nurtured, and set free in the wild. These topics are their babies. They watch them either flourish or fail, and then they review the tapes like football coaches.

Some rounds that didn't go well still haunt them. Brian had high hopes for Fictional Creatures, for instance. He imagined a world of crossover monster fights: Yeti puns against Bigfoot puns, with Dracula and Godzilla tussling not far behind. It did not go that way at all. The contestants argued *all* fictional characters are technically fictional creatures. Frasier Crane is a fictional creature. Ditto the cast of the Fast and Furious octilogy. And even when the punsters stayed on track, there were other problems. After someone made a pun about witches, people in the audience complained that witches are real, citing a wealth of affable Wiccans.

"They had a problem with that one," Brian says. "Yet they *roar* at pedophilia puns."

I'm having a hard time wrapping my head around how involved a process they've made this into. It should be so much easier. It certainly is at Punderdome. I search my brain for a potential new topic and come up with one instantly.

"What about, like, Explorers?"

Everyone's faces stretch and constrict with consideration. Over Gary's shoulder, a sandpiper lands inside a terra-cotta birdbath. David digs into the tortilla chips and queso that have just arrived, a faraway look in his eyes.

"Well," Brian says, diplomatically, making a little fort with his fingers, "we'd be willing to accept Meriwether, and Lewis and Clark, and Louisiana Purchase, and—"

"I bought a stainless steel sports car on eBay," David cuts in, waggling his salt-and-pepper eyebrows. "I had to *pounce de leon*."

I have no idea what this means.

"There could be something here," Gary says. "It's not just names of explorers, it's also the Pinta, Niña, and Santa Maria."

"And it's the best we could af*ford*," David says. When nobody reacts to his pun for the second time in a row, he clarifies: "Ford Explorer."

"All right, but let me ask you a question," Brian says as I reach for a tortilla, his eyes narrowed into pizza dough perforations. "Is your *arm strong* enough to lift that chip?"

I drop the chip as though I've been caught shoplifting and it submerges into queso like quicksand.

"Neil Armstrong," Brian continues. "You're telling me he wasn't an explorer? You son of a bitch. He was an American hero. You're not gonna take him?"

His deadpan is chillingly convincing. I know Brian's not actually being hostile right now, but I only kind of know that and also he is not smiling one iota.

"Well, I guess—"

"Oh, you *are* gonna take him? Are you gonna take every astronaut? Or are you gonna decide, on your own stinking set of values, who's an explorer in the astronaut program?"

"And then there's fictional explorers," Gary points out.

"Dora the Explorer."

"Microsoft Internet," Brian says. "Explorer? You make the call."

His pointy finger is now two inches away from my sternum. At the next table over, a guy with Navajo braids and John Lennon sunglasses is staring at me while vaping.

"Yeah, that's a tough one," I concede.

The guiding principle here seems to be that the contestants are all high-level pun hackers, out to exploit any weakness the planning committee might have left exposed. My hosts are like grizzled war veterans who return from combat and trust nobody back in civilian life, every garbage can a potential IED.

Books and Authors isn't possible because the punsters could just make up the name of any author—and even if they didn't, it's "too broad." Perhaps there's a category so broad it would never run out, at which point we'd all give up and make a new life of it in the backyard behind O. Henry's old house.

"Couldn't you just steer them the right way when they get too granular?" I ask.

"We do that," Gary says. "It just gets tricky sometimes. But they wouldn't have this problem at Punderdome, because there's a finite amount of time to come up with stuff and present it and they can only go on for so long."

I want to remind them that they are, in fact, the organizing committee and that they definitely have the power to enforce any arbitrary time limit they want, and maybe let the audience decide the winner with a clap-off. I get the feeling, though, that asking why they don't make the O. Henry more like Punderdome would freeze this table into an icy tundra.

Just as I'm spiraling, Brian starts laughing like a loon and bolts out of his chair. Two women with matching side mullets and Day-Glo sunglasses look at us. The source of laughter quickly becomes clear. David has a gelatinous dollop of queso on his forehead and he is unaware of it. He remains unaware of it even after Brian takes a picture with his phone and shows it to him, right up until Brian points a finger directly at the splash of cheese sauce on David's forehead in the photo.

"Okay, let's talk through a topic I've been wanting to bring up," David says, abruptly changing the subject as he wipes down his reddening face. "What about Detectives?"

"I like the appeal of it," Brian says. "But I think it's too hard to police because it encompasses movies, books, and TV shows, and the actors who play all those roles."

"You said 'police,'" I point out, but David talks right over me.

"I didn't ask you how you would shoot it down," he spits back. "Let's discuss it."

"I'm not shooting it down, but it might be too difficult to enforce."

"But couldn't we say that about anything? About chemistry?"

"A book about chemistry doesn't grow weekly with more popular culture being expanded," Brian says, on a roll. "I could do a quick Google and come up with a hundred detectives you've never heard of—you can't come up with a hundred elements nobody knows."

"But saying 'there's too many' can apply to *any* topic."

Brian's entire head becomes the kind of Herculean eye roll glimpsed in many a reaction gif.

"Okay: Detectives," he says, scrunching up his lips. "So we take the names of detectives, obviously. Is Jethro Gibbs of *CSI* a detective? He's an investigator for the military."

Somehow, I remember that Jethro Gibbs is Mark Harmon's character on *NCIS*, not *CSI*, but I would rather stick my head in a microwave than point that out right now.

"I would take it because it's slower to not take it," David says.

"So already we're taking something because it's a hassle not to? And speaking of hassle, is *Knight Rider* David Hasselhoff a detective? Hey, I happen to be friends with a detective, does he count?"

"We could also just do Names of Detectives," David says, crossing his arms.

"We're not taking the names of the movies?"

"Only if the character is in the name of the movie."

A royal flush smile spreads across Brian's face.

"So let me get this right. This is the category," Brian says and lets it breathe for a moment. "Names of Detectives, Also Movies, But Only If in Title. That's a winner right there. I wanna sit with a beer and watch that one play out."

"All right, fine! No Detectives!" David says, bolting out of his seat. I now have no problem at all visualizing the pun scrimmages these two must have had back in the day.

Gary catches the dizzy, demoralized look on my face from across the table and raises an eyebrow.

"We sure know how to suck the fun out of puns, don't we?"

BY THE TIME I leave Spider House, my head is spinning. Not only am I seeing pun possibilities in every printed word I pass, which has been my brain's modus operandi lately, I'm also zooming out and grouping words in categories and debating whether they'd fly as O. Henry topics. I just want to go to a meadow somewhere for a while and decompress, maybe think about clouds and how fluffy they are. If being around nonstop puns for a couple hours has this effect on me, what's it going to be like soaking inside of them for an entire day, and competing against people who thrive in such harsh conversational climates? I had to admit, though, as weird and intense as things had just gotten, it hadn't been boring.

On the way back to my friend's apartment, near the chrome chicken trailer and the wax castle, I see dozens of people gathered on the bridge commonly known as Bat Bridge. This time, I do ask what's happening. It turns out people come here every day, often around dusk, because that's when an entire galaxy of bats swarm out from beneath the bridge and paint the sky with their collective mass. Amazingly, these things that are so hor-rifying individually somehow shed their hideousness as they increase in number and transform into sheer spectacle.

One of something awful is just awful, but thousands of something awful is something you just have to see. In its own Austin-weird way, it's beautiful.

# 4

## SPITTING THE LOTTO TICKET

During a break in December's Punderdome, Words Nightmare looks up from her phone and catches me snooping. I pretend to be mesmerized by the DJ booth over her shoulder—*What song will he play next?!*—and that I'm definitely not checking out whether her fervent thumb-flicks are footprints on a Tinder-sprint.

When I stop pretending and look back, her dark eyebrows are raised expectantly, pushing up her uneven fringe. Words Nightmare, a former ergonomic engineer turned freelance writer, whose real name is Ally Spier, has busted me. The crowd noise around us seems to fizzle as I sink into low-grade shame.

"Are you wondering if there are any good matches in this room?" she asks, finally.

"Yes, very much," I say.

Although I first saw Ally at the *New York Post* Punder-dome a few months ago, where she enchanted the crowd and tied with Jerzy for the win, I've only met her once since then, for coffee. It seems a little early in our knowing each other to talk best practices for geolocational dating apps. Perhaps there's something about seeing someone at their most vulnerable, though—in a freestyle pun juggle—that facilitates level jumping.

"No good matches tonight," she announces. "Usually guys message me later, 'Did I see you at Punderdome?' And I prefer that because then it's like we could've conceivably met here, but without the awkwardness of actually meeting here."

Ally has big black glasses like a 1950s waitress, and a thrift store raider's fashion sense, with unpredictable combinations of layers. She talks fast and makes jokes so deadpan-chipper, you don't realize a joke has been made until a moment later. One of Ally's Tinder profile photos depicts her onstage, smiling just after landing a killer pun, the crowd receiving it like a Southern Baptist church choir. A lot of suitors comment on the picture, using it as an excuse to reach out. Punderdome isn't just a catalyst in her love life, though, it's also a barometer.

"Because Punderdome is something that's become a part of my life in a couple different ways, I will now introduce it as this thing—'Here's something I do, you're obviously invited'—and nobody has objected," she says. "But if anyone ever did object, I'd say we're done, right now. That's it."

Punning must be among the world's least likely aphrodisiacs, somewhere between oysters and the parking lot of any Dunkin' Donuts, but it is. I've seen it happen. Later that night, a young woman with blue hair approaches Jerzy, making unmistakable sexy eyes. "You're literally amazing," she tells him, and then walks away. I'm not sure whether she means "literally" as a meta-pun or not.

Once she's gone, I give Jerzy a very serious look and ask point-blank: "Are there pun groupies?"

"Kind of, yeah," he says, shrugging. "That's why they call it Punder-*do me*."

At any given Punderdome, a player who does well might get complimented or outright hit on once or twice, usually during the break or after the show ends. It's happened to Tim. It's happened to Isaac. It's happened to pretty much all the women of Punderdome. One night, the Littlefield DJ passed Jerzy a note from a mystery woman, simply stating "*you make me corny*." People who are into puns are apparently way into them.

"It's not just that there's potential sex to be had," Jerzy says. "It's cool because ordinarily if you're the person making a pun in a room, you're probably always that guy or that girl. But at a pun competition, it's a room *full of* that guy and that girl. So basically, while a pun can waylay a conversation, if you're with a bunch of people who also make puns, it can get you way laid."

There is no way he invented that line just for my benefit.

Eventually, the competition builds to a final round between Ally and a guy who goes by Daft Pun. He's thin, wolfishly handsome, and he looks like the star of every student film ever submitted in good faith to a major film festival. I've seen Daft Pun before, back at the *New York Post* event, though at the time he had on a tinfoil hat like an alien truther, and he was part of a duo. His name is Nikolai Vanyo, he's a music video and film director a few years out of college, and he is close with Ally. Tonight, the two friends engage in a fast-paced pun-off and when Nikolai wins, it's his first time doing so without his teammate. Ally takes the defeat with grace, clapping for Nikolai as he steps forward, arms out, to embrace the crowd's love.

Punderdome is officially over for the year.

WE'VE NOW REACHED the pun solstice, the verbal equinox. The O. Henry Pun-Off is six months away, a comfortably far-off X in next year's calendar. That's five more Punderdomes for anyone who plans on heading to Austin in the spring. My performance at the December Dome was an improvement so marginal it would take nanotechnology to track it, but if I keep going back, I'm bound to get better. There's just one problem. Fred Firestone gets frostbite even thinking about New York in the winter, so he stays home in St. Louis each January and February, during which time there is no Punderdome. Tumbleweeds will be scraping across the cold ground of the northern metropolitan pun community for months. The circus has left town.

Competitive wordplay doesn't evaporate in the off-season, though. Just because the Olympics aren't returning for three years, the athletes don't automatically abandon their draconian workouts to binge-watch *Buffy the Vampire Slayer*. There had to be options for practicing beyond just jamming puns into any conversational crevice they almost fit. I was going to find them.

Picture someone practicing for a pun competition. It's the saddest *Rocky* training montage of all, isn't it? In my case, the image entails a man firmly in his midthirties, sitting alone in his bedroom with the door shut, making puns about colors. ("Is having the blues what made Matthew *Perry wrinkle*?") The thought of my dead relatives and pets looking down from another plane of existence as I do this is mortifying.

I start off with an overly generous five-minute limit. It's just a warm-up, something to get my brain used to rattling off puns in a hurry until I can do it instantaneously. Speed is key. Speed is the killer app of pun competitions. You have to be bullet-quick. Not just quick in the way of a devastating comeback when someone insults you—say, for devoting too much time to pun calisthenics—but so quick you already have another pun lined up right away and one after that. Punning is like chess that way: it gets tougher with a time constraint, you've got to think far ahead, and nobody looks cool doing it. When you receive the topic, Colors, you peruse the Pantone catalog in your brain, pull *powder blue,* think "I had some cocaine but my *powder blew* away," and on to the next, tout de suite.

I text Ally about sending over some categories she remembers from Punderdomes past, and the laundry list she delivers should be enough to sustain several practice sessions. I set my iPhone to stopwatch, put five minutes on the clock, and glance at the first topic on Ally's list. It's Feminism. Go!

The words *slut walk* are the first that pop in my head. That is probably not good news for me as a person. Next is *suffragette.* I can take a plane but I will not *suffer a jet.* Okay! *Breast cancer awareness* appears and there's nothing I can or should do with that. Then there's Harriet Beecher Stowe, the famed abolitionist. Her existence was a coup for feminism, right? I probably should have skipped this topic.

At the end of five minutes, I have a bunch of prompts, but only two puns that might go over well at Punderdome: "Lumberjacks get birth control from *Plaid Parenthood,*" and "I mix up parts of the couch because I'm *intersectional.*" Did I mention it took me five minutes to come up with these? A short while later, I realize I could've wedged "mans*plane*" into a line about suffering a jet, which would've been pretty sweet if I'd thought of it in the moment, in front of a crowd, and not alone, sprawled across my bed, the only audience my cat and whichever NSA spy is assigned to my MacBook camera.

Not everybody needs to do this. Some punsters are pure naturals, proficient without practice. The very first time Rekha

Shankar entered Punderdome and competed as Punky Brewster, for instance, she won. Then she kept coming back and kept winning. Sometimes, on weekends, she would illustrate two-panel pun comics on her blog—as a challenge to regularly create share-worthy wordplay—and that's about as close as she got to formally practicing. Rekha considers the work she does spot-pitching ideas for funny videos on MTV News and ClickHole to be practice enough.

Other people put in a maximal effort. Ben Ziek poured a lot of hours into becoming the Final Boss of pun competitions. The first year he competed in the O. Henry, Ziek prepared for Punslingers by creating a PowerPoint that pulled topics at random. He rigged it to display categories for five seconds at a time, the screen flashing a stop sign eventually. Ziek took on these topics over and over, pushing his mind to excrete its boundless stores of trivia and puns until doing so became a reflex. It was not a skill that endeared him to many other people out in the world.

Earlier this year, Jerzy Gwiazdowski and his brother Jordan, a.k.a. A Little Kick in the Punt, developed their own unique method of practicing: a podcast.

Jordan, who is four years Jerzy's junior, is an actor with a nasally voice that often unexpectedly veers into an old-timey auctioneer's or a cartoon squirrel's. He moved to New York in 2013 from the Gwiazdowski home base of Milwaukee, where he'd felt creatively cockblocked. Before arriving in his brother's adopted city of a decade, Jordan had no interest in punning—not until tagging along at Punderdome one night to see what Jerzy had been hyping up during Christmas visits. He quickly found himself enjoying the competition, one of many performative outlets he had discovered in the city—along with a series of impromptu dramatic scenes set in a bar, and the kind of experimental theater pieces that require full-frontal nudity. He kept going back to Punderdome with Jerzy, and he kept improving. ("I took him on as my padawan," is how Jerzy tells it.) Jordan's acting career also got a boost around the same time, when his low-key doppelgänger, Adam Driver, became a huge star. Then came the podcast.

You'll notice there are not a lot of pun-based podcasts. Despite the fact that podcast categories have begun to reach Rule 34–level diversification, the demand for pun content in this medium has been less than robust. The Gwiazdowskis didn't set out to contribute to it either. When they considered starting a comedy podcast, though, they couldn't agree on any idea until they randomly recorded some practice sessions for the 2015 O. Henry. That's when *Punk Assed: A Puncast* was born. Although the formal practice didn't help either brother actually defeat Ziek at the Pun-Off—Jordan had the misfortune of going up against him in the first round—they both enjoyed these recording sessions so much they looked into whether anybody else was putting out a pun podcast. Nobody was.

Each episode of *Punk Assed* offers a series of pun games and the odd lesson on great punsters in history. Once the brothers got a few episodes under their belts, they quickly noticed that the show had a side effect of keeping them more primed for Punderdome than ever. They'd built in a surefire incentive to practice each week, and the effort showed. Since Jerzy and Jordan started recording, the two have faced off in the final round at Punderdome several times. Although the podcast audience remained modest, the two are committed to putting out *Punk Assed* as they gear up for the 2016 O. Henry, where they expect their pun-superpowers will carry the day.

As the Punderdome hibernation months began, though, the

Gwiazdowskis found the format of the podcast was getting a little stale. They decided to freshen it up with some new voices, by throwing a party that would double as a recording session. They invited some Brooklyn punsters to the studio for beer, pizza, and pun games. I couldn't say yes fast enough.

"This is going to be brutal," says Max Parke, a hulking, Vandyke-bearded friend of Jerzy's, who looks like a really tall hobbit. "You guys are internationally ranked punsters. It's like if Picabo Street invited me to go skiing."

"It's not a competition, we're just messing around." Jerzy says. "Nice pull on Picabo Street, though."

We're inside Front/Pearl Studio, which is actually a basement loft on a cobblestone street corner in DUMBO. It belongs to Jerzy's friend, Trevor, a bearded actor in a newsie cap with a wily smile. Just beyond the sparsely furnished parlor is an alcove Trevor has converted into a studio space. The room's centerpiece is a small stage he built out of reclaimed wood from the Coney Island boardwalk, and atop that stage rests a drum set and speakers. The band Beirut used to practice here, I'm told more than once, as though whatever audio alchemy launched Beirut into the Coachellasphere is perhaps lingering in the exposed brick. It smells like patchouli oil and cedarwood and the faintest trace of basement musk. A mishmash of blankets has been arranged in front of the stage, big enough that it could easily accommodate a large picnic or orgy. We're just waiting for a couple more people before we get started.

Aside from Trevor and the Gwiazdowskis, there's Melton, a novice punster with a middle school student's wispy mustache, and Max, a computer programmer who has been grinding it out at Punderdome for years but has made only modest progress. Homestar Punner, a.k.a. Sam Corbin, is a Punderdome star who is supposed to be here but is running late. A couple other actorly friends accepted the invitation out of sheer curiosity. They don't quite know what is about to happen.

Jerzy and Jordan are hunched over at opposite ends of the room like twin rooftop gargoyles, scribbling pun challenges on their notepads, pizza grease coagulating on the surface of untouched slices nearby. Jerzy is wearing a long-sleeve V-neck and fuzzy blue socks; Jordan has a camo hoodie pulled over a baseball cap, and his fingernails are painted shiny black. They look less like brothers than most brothers.

In the kitchen, Trevor is making me a drink: cherry moonshine with hellfire bitters. As he mixes it together, he produces a tiny bottle plugged with a medicine dropper. The label has a green lightning bolt running down the side.

"Are you 420?" he asks.

"He means 'Are you four and twenty blackbirds,'" Jerzy says, without looking up.

"Oh, I thought he meant, like, 'Are you ten Jackie Robinsons,'" I say. The movie, *42*, came out recently; otherwise, I'd never have known Robinson's number.

Clearly, nobody needs it explained that 420 is a shibboleth of pot friendliness. If you made a Venn diagram of the average Punderdomer and the archetypal stoner, I assume it would resemble the circumference of a bong's rim. This is the first I'm seeing it firsthand, but it's something I've wondered about: Does getting high elevate punsters to some cosmic plane of thought, a rocketship to the northernmost stars in the lexical galaxy, or does it guarantee a failure to launch? I'm about to find out. Trevor puts a few drops of pot bitters in my drink, and it tastes like a dank licorice slushie. Here we go, away with words.

Jordan reports that Homestar Punner might not be arriving for a while, so we should just start without her. Everybody files in front of the stage and starts arranging themselves across the blankets. Trevor takes a seat at his stageside organ while Jerzy and Jordan fiddle with their recording equipment.

"After making thirty episodes of the podcast together, we're looking to spice things up in the bedroom," Jerzy says.

That's where we come in. Our presence adds the pressure of an audience, but also, the brothers hope, the load-bearing weight of collaboration. When any of us has an idea, we are encouraged to say it into the microphone.

Soon, Jordan hits Record and the show begins, just as the first languid waves of pot tranquility lap at my brain. The idea of speaking suddenly seems like an impossibility.

The most elemental game the Gwiazdowskis play on the podcast is called Bro Pun Says We, which takes me far too long to realize is a pun on Open Sesame. The two give themselves ninety seconds to come up with puns on a topic—well, officially ninety seconds, but more like a few minutes—and then go back and forth until they run out of steam. Usually, Jordan rolls a D&D twenty-sided die to pick a numbered topic from the PUNY page, but tonight, they throw the question out to us. Melton suggests: Mammals.

"*Rocky 4* is my favorite movie I ever saw *Dolph in*," says Jerzy.

"That's *gorilla* good Dolph movie," Jordan says, kneeling in a b-boy pose. "Can you think of any *otter* ones?"

Max yells out "*Rats!*" and nobody reacts. "You know, like as a one-liner?"

I ransack my mind for mammals, but punnable ones are suddenly an endangered species. The image of an ape appears and so much time goes by without a pun occurring to me, I'm eventually just looking at an ape with my mind's eye, waiting for him to do something cool. Then I move on to dinosaurs. Right as the category collapses, at the exact moment Jordan asks if anybody needs a rimjob since he's around to *blow holes,* I finally feel confident enough to shout something out.

"This old guy asked me if those Jurassic-era beasts were mammals and I said '*Daaah, I-don't-know, sir.*'"

The pot has definitely kicked in.

"Oh, wow—from left field!" Jordan says, rubbing the bridge of his nose. "Also: Not a mammal!"

"Yeah, but that's why I said I didn't know," I clarify.

"Speaking of prehistoric mammals," Jerzy says. "Max is looking like one over there with his *woolly man-mouth.*"

Everybody cheers and Trevor lays down some organ thunder. Through my haze, the melodic soundtrack lends the whole experience a surreal, silent movie aura.

The next game has a lot of history. Jerzy and Jordan used to play it as kids on long car rides with their father. There's also a similar improv exercise called 185. A certain number of somethings walk into a bar—in the improv exercise, it's 185; for Jordan and Jerzy, it's 99—and the bartender refuses to serve them. The somethings then offer a punny retort. At present, the somethings are ducks, although everyone is encouraged to yell a new topic when the current one runs out of steam.

"Ninety-nine ducks walk into a bar," Jerzy starts. "The bartender says, 'We don't serve ducks here,' and the ducks say, 'Oh, but you're *down* with geese?'"

These jokes would be hard to execute, stone sober. As is, my mind is like one of those stuffed-animal grabber machines; the metallic claw fumbling inside of a word cloud, suffixes and syllables spilling out of its clutches, so many quarters eaten. Sometimes a pun dances on the tip of my tongue and disappears like a lost sneeze. I stay silent, and nobody else interrupts the brothers' flow for a long stretch.

When the topic turns to pro wrestlers, Melton clears his throat.

"Ninety-nine pro wrestlers . . . walk into a bar and the bartender says . . . 'We don't serve you.' So one of the wrestlers goes, 'Have you *Cena* John?'"

The difference in delivery between the Gwiazdowskis on-stage and Max, Melton, and myself in the crowd is pronounced enough to be its own category of sonic. We three lesser punsters speak very deliberately, like we're just learning the language, feeling out how the words might syllabically hang together, and desperately trying to mold them into a joke. Meanwhile, Jerzy and Jordan generally sound like they're reciting polished material from a script. With this golden-hued delivery, Jerzy can do a wrestling pun that hinges on, "Can you smell what the *Rockettes* cooking?" and still sell it all the way.

"Not serving wrestlers? *WWF,* man?" Trevor yells from his perch at the organ.

After a few minutes, I'm still struggling to grasp the structure of this game, but I decide to give it a go. My lone contribution is convoluted nonsense.

"Ninety-nine pro wrestlers walk into a bar and immediately meet a woman named Jessica," I say, boldly disregarding the bartender's role in the joke. "The wrestlers start talking to Jessica and she asks, 'Do you ever get hurled through the air?' And they say, *'Jessie, the body venture-a.'*"

Actual silence. Room tone. I can practically hear the hiss on the recording as air whooshes gently against the microphone. Sometimes only part of a word can be used for a pun, and then the rest of it just hangs there, like a remainder in long division. These kinds of puns are usually the least funny, and this one has other problems as well. When I listen to the podcast later, I'm glad this part has been cut. I decide to keep quiet for a while. Maybe if I just sit back and absorb, I'll catch a contact pun-high and start throwing down some serious heat.

Despite the fact that the pot hasn't made me more creative so much as it's installed a floating hall of mirrors in my head, when Trevor circulates a small glass pipe, I absorb that, too.

The air in the room seems to lighten after Homestar Punner arrives. Sam's a playwright and editor with curious eyes, a mop of messy blond locks, and a hair-trigger laugh. She's way closer to the Gwiazdowskis' level than the rest of us, with a dedication to punning that goes far beyond the Dome. Lately, Sam has been experimenting with pun-based performance art. One piece she staged in Central Park involved Sam dancing around in a bear suit to a song by the band Grizzly Bear while a friend held up a sign that read BEAR WITH US. Then her friend flipped the sign around so that it became BARE WITH US, and she stripped down to a flesh-colored suit and bared her soul. Some of the passersby would get angry and yell. Others would clap. One guy talked to them about Jesus, but he probably would've done that anyway had there been no bear puns.

Jerzy and Jordan abandon the stage and join the rest of the group in a circle on top of the blankets, placing the microphone stand in the center. The next wave of games begins with Headlines. It's something Jerzy cooked up after he and Words Nightmare beat the editors of the *New York Post* at Punderdome. One of the brothers reads a bizarre story from the day's news and we all come up with headlines for it. Something about the addition of Sam and the human feng shui we've just done makes everyone less shy about jumping in.

The first story involves a man accused of assaulting his girlfriend after she wouldn't smell his armpit. There is a lot to unpack here: brands of deodorant, body parts, the simple act of stinking. Sam yells, "*Underarm Her*," and crooks her elbow in the air to demonstrate. Trevor adopts a Mr. T voice and croaks out, "I *pit-y* the fool" from his organ seat. Jerzy says "Law and *Odor*." The room soon ruptures with ideas that abandon the Headlines structure, and each produces aftershocks of laughter.

"The girlfriend is now under twenty-four-hour protection," Sam says.

"Because, man, he was really sweating her."

"'I swear I'm in here for trying to get my girlfriend to smell my armpit,'" I say, a pleading tone to my voice. "'*Right, guard?*'"

What we're all building may be epically pointless and ephemeral—an inside joke that never catches on, a loud parade through a ghost town—but I am nonetheless fully invested in helping it come together. We're feeding off one another's energy and riding the lingual wave together. Maybe it's because we're standing around in a circle, like a breakdancing crew, but this party is starting to feel like a gang initiation ritual. I briefly imagine another group of punsters preparing to battle us in an abandoned warehouse downtown, stunting through the streets like Michael Jackson's *Bad* video. Apparently, I'm still stoned.

The cerebral starburst when a pun epiphany hits the group and everyone starts laughing, though, is its own high. During a break, Max complains about his neighbors blaring high-octane

EDM while he tries to watch TV late at night. Sam blurts out, "That's so *ravin'.*" Everyone dies laughing. This is the Hellenic ideal of what a pun can do. That moment when the elements are right there, then someone ties them together and spits the lotto ticket—it's addictive. You see it in movies and shows, like when the guys in *The 40-Year-Old Virgin* are riffing on a penis cake pan, and Steve Carell comes up with "Betty *Cocker.*" Playing pun games like these, without the competition, feels like we're always on the edge of that moment. But then there's the opposite moment, the feeling of coming up short while riffing in a group and ruining the rhythm. You see moments like this in pop culture, too, like when Ricky Gervais tries to think of a dessert pun to follow "It's just a *trifling* matter" in *The Office* and can only hem and haw. I try not to think about how that possibility is always lurking.

One of the headlines is about an off-duty Florida cop who was fired for jumping onstage at a death metal show in full uniform. After almost every option is exhausted, Jerzy says, "We need to *guitar* police force in gear."

"That's so old. You can't just do that one over and over," Jordan says. "'*Guitar* asses in gear?' It's been used and used. We said we were gonna start calling each other out on this stuff."

The more puns that cross the transom of your brainpan, the more you have stockpiled, forever on deck. They become like those canned anecdotes we all have, spring-loaded and ready to go whenever someone mentions anything related to a certain topic. If you spend time trying to remember your favorite puns while the clock is ticking at Punderdome, rather than make up new ones, it will backfire, but some old standards just become part of your vocabulary. Hear these pun-hacks enough, though, and they lodge in your ear like hocked loogies.

"Are we gonna start keeping track of everything we say?" Jerzy says.

"I'm just saying, if *guitar* is used one more time, you're fired from the podcast."

The next game we play is every bit as complicated as 99 Somethings, only it's a play on the creaky Yiddish joke about finding a fly in one's soup. The brothers have christened this game with the singularly reprehensible pun, He Ain't Heavy, He's My *Broth*-er.

"Waiter, there are boots in my soup," Jordan says.

"Why don't I call the sous chef over—*heel* deal with it," Jerzy shoots back.

We spend a long stretch finding shoes and then cars in a supernaturally large bowl of soup. For some reason, probably having to do with tetrahydrocannabinol, I continue making car puns long after we move on. I spend multiple turns in a row trying in earnest to fashion a joke around Ford Lincoln Mercury—"I can't *af-ford leek in, more curry*"—but it is just not happening. When I listen back later on, I pray that I stay quiet for a bit afterward. I do not. Instead, I keep steering back to my apparent favorite subject: The automobile industry.

"Are you from Detroit?" Max asks.

This is the second way puns can be objectively Bad: timing. You could come up with the greatest wordplay in the world, but if it's a pun about what everybody was talking about five minutes ago, it's too late. The world has moved on. A late pun makes everybody who witnessed its birth imagine the effort expended on it—which feels about as uncomfortably intimate as seeing your friend's parents at the moment of conception. The timing rule also applies to situational appropriateness, which is why historically very few puns are made at funerals.

Suddenly, I can't shake the feeling that everybody here fucking hates me. It seems irrational, but *is it*? When Jordan announces that there's a musical instrument in his soup, Sam responds, "I think Joe left it there, we'd better *ban-Joe*," which feels like a personal attack.

"I guess we'll have to *guitar* selves more soup, mother-fucker!" Jerzy says, looking Jordan dead in the eye.

Everybody laughs and I realize through the cloak of resin coating my thoughts that nobody is thinking about me. They're thinking of puns.

The final game of the night is the same as the first, Bro Pun Says We, except this time with Women's Names instead of Mammals. Jordan passes out paper and we all take a couple minutes to write down puns. As we do so, Trevor lightly strums a ukulele and sings. His voice is actually breathtaking.

"I'm gonna kick this off with a philosophical question about *The Lion King*," Jordan says. "Did *Scar-let* Mufasa die?"

Instead of yelling in the general direction of the microphone stand, as we did before, now we're passing the mic around. After each person speaks into it, there's always a couple hands waggling to get it next, with the most insistent ones winning.

"When I do an ab workout," Sam starts, her hands on her midsection, "I make sure to hold my *core-in*."

"I used to wear an S, and then an M, but now I *rock L*," I say.

"Hey, wanna go to the *bar, brah*?" Jerzy says.

Even though I just went, my hand starts shaking like a grand mal seizure, and Jerzy passes the mic back to me.

"I heard the bar was kind of full, we may have to *jostle in*," I say, and it hits like a battle rap diss, with cascading applause.

This is the closest I've gotten to the back and forth of the final round at Punderdome. Although I started with a handful of ideas written down, those went quickly, and I was happily surprised by how many more kept coming to me.

"I don't like when people successfully prevail because of bullshit," Sam says. "Nobody should *win-on-a* technicality."

"I got kind of high on the way to deliver gifts to the magi," I say, "and I brought frankincense, *myrrh and, uh* . . . I don't know what else."

We then proceed to do the remaining *Sex and the City* character names and call it a night. It's 1:30 in the morning. We have been punning for over four hours.

I leave the basement loft no longer high, but giddy from the group rush of linguistic discovery. We'd chased our categories as far as they could go, mostly free from the time restrictions of competition. There could be no better way to start training in the off-season.

Now that I'd paid way too much attention to what was happening in my head while punning, though, I was curious to find out what was going on in everybody else's.

# Second Round

# 5

## THE PUNNING LINGUISTS

There cannot be enough humor research conferences in the world to require the specificity of a North East Texas Humor Research Conference. As far as I can tell, when entering coordinates into Google Maps, "North East Texas" isn't even a real place. In fact, exactly as few such conferences exist as one might expect. The name turns out to be the organizers' idea of a humor-joke. Wocka-wocka.

What I quickly learn upon arriving is that a humor research conference is among Earth's least funny places. If trying to explain a joke is like dissecting a frog, as E. B. White said, being here is like walking through an endless M. C. Escher house drenched in frog entrails.

I've come here in the name of science, in order to find out more about the mental artillery factory responsible for making puns before Punderdome returns in March. I want to know whether an instinct for instant wordplay comes down to nature, nurture, or neither, and whether the study of humor reveals anything about punning. My search for a linguist who could

speak to this topic leads me to Dr. Salvatore Attardo, dean of
humanities at Texas A&M University-Commerce. Dr. Attardo
not only agreed to discuss puns with me, he extended an invitation to attend this conference, where I could also interview
his colleague Dr. Christian Hempelmann, one of the world's
foremost pun experts, and tour the university's humor lab. No
way would I ever turn down an offer to see a humor lab. For all I
knew, it involved a forensic analysis of airplane food, the sexual
audit of a man from Nantucket, people of different races noting
their differences while using a triple-beam balance as a seesaw,
and lab-coated technicians showing dank memes to a monkey.

The next thing I knew, I was driving a rented Ford Focus
down I-30 East and listening to the new Kanye West, which,
incidentally, is loaded with puns.

"I'm drivin' with no winter tires in December

*Skrrt skrrt skrrt* like a private school for women"

The grass along the highway looks bleached of color, as
though any trace of green has been sucked out through a giant subterranean straw. It isn't exactly farm country, but several
houses I pass have little red barns next to them like sidecars.
Mexican restaurants dot the main streets, occasionally accented
with neon sombreros, and the last one I make out before arriving at my hotel is called TaMolly's. (Whomever the "Molly"
refers to in this pun, I hope she's happy with her choices). It's
an omen. I've either come to the right place or it's just that once
you start noticing puns, you realize they're inescapable.

The university campus is sprawling and the map I pull up
on my phone has an intricate number system for buildings and
parking lots. Eventually, after much anxious power walking, I
arrive where I'm supposed to be: the Department of Industrial
Engineering and Technology. It seems like the wrong place to

hear deeply researched theories from leading pun experts, but the conference had to happen somewhere.

The lobby where the reception mixer is held has particleboard ceilings, patchy carpeting that looks like it itches, long couches the precise color of tongue, and artwork like blurry stills from a laser light show. The assistant who registers me also hands over a name tag on a lanyard, along with an itinerary, and a T-shirt commemorating the day. The logo on the itinerary is an armadillo on its back, whose body spells out the initials of the conference. I thought an armadillo on its back was an unambiguous symbol of death, with backwater bozos occasionally known to place a beer in the deceased's claws, but this one appears to be laughing hysterically. Is this another sign?

There's a buffet of warmed-over spring rolls and crab cakes in chafing dishes, resting on a table draped in the school's colors, blue and gold. A group that is diverse in gender, ethnicity, and amount of snow on the rooftop is arranged around it, in varying degrees of casual; mostly dresses and black leggings for the women, and button-downs tucked into jeans for the men. I load up on spring rolls, perch on a tongue-couch, and peruse the itinerary while working up to a state of mingle-readiness.

There's a man with a prodigious gut poking out of a gray suit who appears to pull every crab-cake-gripping attendee into his orbit. Even without seeing his name tag, I sense that this is Dr. Attardo. He has a high forehead with slightly mussed graying hair, and his manner is very serious for someone chairing a humor conference. When I make my way over and introduce myself, Dr. Attardo cordially thanks me for coming, in a glottal accent I peg as possibly Belgian. His demeanor does not soften at all, though, from putting a face to an e-mail correspondence.

Perhaps he's like Jerzy and needs to get in his zone before addressing the crowd.

Soon, Dr. Attardo summons over his colleague, Dr. Hempelmann, so we can iron out our itinerary for the next day. The world-class pun expert, some of whose papers I've read to prepare for this trip, receives me in a slightly warmer manner.

"I hate you for making me wake up at eight thirty on a Saturday," he says.

Dr. Hempelmann has a ruddy complexion, a mild Swedish mullet, and an eccentrically collared deep-blue shirt like a jaunty Bond villain. I have no idea what to say to make an adult feel better about waking up semiearly to talk to me, so instead I mention how excited I am to see the humor lab.

"'Lab' is a bit of an overstatement," he says, and a photographer walking around captures the exact moment I realize just how long this weekend is going to be.

After we confirm the time for tomorrow's sleep-disrupting interview, and which assistant will conduct me around the lab, the conference officially commences. Everybody shuffles into a clown-car-tiny classroom. It is very hot. A series of framed posters on the wall touts the benefits of coffee and most are rather cloying, like "Coffee Tastes Best with a Friend," but then there's one that reads "Coffee Makes You Gay," which during the roughly 867 hours I spend in this classroom over the next two days, nobody appears to notice or react to, making me wonder whether this is, itself, some kind of humor research experiment. After everyone is seated, Dr. Attardo pads over to a podium with a plaque that reads DEPARTMENT OF INDUSTRIAL ENGINEERING AND TECHNOLOGY, but some of the letters in the first word are faded, so it actually reads DIE ART MEN. As everyone's conversations finally fizzle, he addresses the crowd.

"Sorry that we've had to relocate onto campus this year, but the reason we're doing this is simple: I do not look good in a cheerleader outfit."

Everybody laughs and because we are at a humor research conference, I can't help but analyze what has just happened. I think about how Attardo's somber bearing makes it register harder when he says something intended to be funny, apart from just the mental image of him in a cheerleader outfit. I think about the mechanism by which we are all exhaling rapidly through our bronchial passages to communicate that we are amused. I wonder whether anyone else here is analyzing what it means that we are laughing—perhaps including it in a running tally—and whether they do this all the time, the sound of guffaws triggering abstract calculations.

The dean follows up with a "But seriously" and then explains that a cheerleading competition booked up the hotel they usually hold the conference in, hence why we are here instead, in this small classroom together.

Once the keynote is finished and the first presentations begin, the cheerleader joke ends up being the last laugh I experience for some time. Each successive presentation, spoken in near-impenetrable academese, is an attempt to prove things everybody already knows and nobody really cares about. There's the one whose thesis is that irony is not inherently funny, especially to young children, and there's another that makes a cohesive scientific argument that *The Onion*'s headlines are, in fact, awesome. The latter presenter, a Ph.D. student in applied linguistics, uses a laser pointer to highlight some entries from his corpus of *Onion* headlines, even though the projection screen is less than a foot away. This corpus is only the first of the weekend's many, many corpuses—or as another presenter calls them, *corpora*. All of them seem statistically insignificant, though, especially the corpus of stand-up comedy one guy made out of transcripts from fifteen comedy albums—the only ones he professed to be able to find. (Fact: At least fifteen comedy albums came out last month, whatever month you're reading this.) I don't know much about professional humor research, but I do know that fifteen albums do not a corpus make.

Each presentation is twenty-five minutes long, with five minutes reserved for questions afterward. When the speaker has five minutes left, a woman up front helpfully holds up signs that read "5," then eventually "1," and finally "Stop!" Whenever the last one is flashed, it reminds me of when stand-up comics get the red light and have to wrap up their set. I keep waiting for a presenter to say "That's my time" and go hit on people at the bar, in true stand-up comedian fashion.

During the questions portion, the same guy always kicks the tires on everybody's presentation with questions that more than once begin, "I'm just gonna play devil's advocate here . . ." His name is Carey, he's skinny and bald, with squirrelly eyes, and his vibe could best be described as several concurrent cocaine epiphanies. I keep thinking he had better have something amazing when it's his turn, the way he keeps poking holes in everyone else's presentations. Tomorrow, he will be the one who put together the corpus of stand-up comedy. Until then, there are many more presentations to get through, and their net effect is that it begins to feel as though humor has not only been inspected and autopsied but fully eradicated, as though we're studying a relic from some long-dead civilization. Was I, or anyone I've known, ever actually funny? Was anything?

FRESHLY SHOWERED AND continentally breakfasted, I arrive on campus the next morning for the designated pre–9:00 A.M. pun chat—the whole reason I've come to Dallas. The conference surrounding it is starting to feel like a slow-motion car wreck that turns me into rhetorical roadkill, another armadillo. The experience has only made the inner workings of puns feel more unknowable. I'm now desperate to learn anything.

Attardo is on the phone in the administrative office, so I go to the pantry and pour myself a cup of orange-tinted coffee from a prehistoric hotplate. By the time I return to the lobby, Dr. Hempelmann has materialized, wearing the same shirt with the same strange collar as the previous day, and looking slightly more rumpled and red-faced. My time with the world-class pun expert is already dwindling, so I start the interview while Attardo is out of the room.

"Is there anything in people's upbringing that might make them good at puns?" I ask Dr. Hempelmann, who is now plunked down on a couch, rubbing his temples.

All the champions I've met over the past few months seem to have had overlapping formative experiences that foreshadowed their pun proficiency.

Jerzy and Jordan grew up playing Scrabble with three generations of punsters in their family.

Ben Ziek devoured crossword puzzles and riddle books as a child, when he wasn't watching game shows.

Ariel was the eleventh-best speller in California when she was in middle school, and she carried Bananagrams with her everywhere she went.

Isaac was another spelling bee kingpin, and so were Tim and Ally. Tim was also addicted to the word game Balderdash, but he got bored with the prompts on the cards eventually and started writing his own.

Ally and Sam were both Daily Jumble junkies.

Almost everybody played word games on long car trips, which I am retroactively jealous of, having grown up in more of a Punch Buggy Blue household. The high incidence rate of Boggle too could not be a coincidence. There had to be a linguistic explanation for what all the champions have in common.

"Maybe their mental lexicon is structured the wrong way?" Dr. Hempelmann says after a while. "Their semantic associations aren't so much semantic but more phonological. Normal people, they hear a word and it's all about the meaning—the sound is completely secondary, it's just a gateway to the meaning. But people who are punsters are constantly tickled by the sound of language. And you should only work with the meaning of language instead, since that's what it's there for."

There is a chance that one of the world's experts on puns actually hates puns.

All I want to know is if there are common characteristics in a punster's upbringing beyond what I've already gathered, and here we've arrived at punning as mental disorder. This sort of thinking has been in vogue lately. The past year has seen an onslaught of news stories about a punning disease called *witzelsucht,* which is German for "addiction to wisecracking." Patients usually present with witzelsucht after having a stroke or incurring other forms of brain damage, leading some critics to conflate all compulsive punning with evidence of a damaged brain. This idea has not exactly had the pun community dancing in the streets.

One of the idea's detractors is Dr. Richard Lederer, a linguist who has written several books on puns and has been barred—in a friendly, respectful way—from competing at the O. Henry Pun-Off, due to his professional leg up. When I talk to Dr. Lederer, weeks after the conference, he is emphatic about wordplay being a sign of intelligence rather than a mental aberration. Despite the fact that his livelihood depends on the idea that he's right, his argument holds water. While the poor soul who literally cannot stop punning even for a moment might suffer from an affliction such as witzelsucht, according to Dr. Lederer, the average person putting disparate words and phrases together is basically doing hammer-kicks at a cranial CrossFit. Nobody in the world has yet laid eyes upon the brain scan of a person in the middle of a pun competition, but Lederer hypothesizes that doing so would reveal a brain that looks like it's on fire. (But, like, a good fire.)

Dr. Attardo is now back and hurriedly putting out a donut and coffee spread.

"This may be more of a question for a neuroscientist, but assuming no mental disorder, what goes on inside a person's head when they make a pun?" I ask.

Dr. Hempelmann, who looks thoroughly unthrilled to be here, considers for a moment and then announces, "You'd probably have to ask a neuroscientist."

I'm about to scream into the nearest couch cushion and ask if anyone knows the linguistic implications of why I'm doing that, when Dr. Attardo, probably sensing that his colleague's answer could have been a touch more expansive, sets aside the napkins he's neatly stacking and clears his throat.

"Basically, here's what the neuroscientist will tell you," he says. "A good way of representing what's in the brain is to think of it as strings of lights on a Christmas tree. So you have one string that's white, and those lights are all the associations of meaning. If you have 'dog,' you have 'puppy' and 'bitch' and all the words that are related to dogs. So that's one string, but then you're going to have another string that's red and it's 'fog,' 'bog,' 'log'—all the associations on the sound and all the sounds that begin the same way. What is happening when you make a pun is that you're kind of crossing the strings of lights."

I picture this happening in my head onstage at Punderdome. I'm frantically trying to decorate a Christmas tree in ninety seconds while an elf sings the Alvin and the Chipmunks Christmas song, pine needles flying everywhere, and with hundreds of people watching. It feels about right. Punning is just tangling up Christmas lights.

When I do eventually talk to a neuroscientist who has devoted time to studying puns, he confirms the accuracy of this description. However, Dr. Vinod Goel is more interested in what happens in children's brains when they hear a pun. Many of the first jokes kids hear and tell each other are actually stealth education bombs alerting them to the existence of alternate meanings for words. When children find out that what's black and white and r-e-a-d all over is a newspaper, their brains explode with verbal aptitude. However, Dr. Goel seems to agree with Dr. Hempelmann about pun appreciation in adults being something like a defect. He contends that while puns are important for children, as people get older, they should make a permanent switch to semantic jokes that depend upon the nonliteral meaning of words and background information. According to Goel, anyone opting for the less sophisticated wordplay that is the bread and butter of pun competitions must be deeply immature. Judging from my experience in the pun world thus far, this diagnosis is hard to argue with. Just this past month, a new competition called the Bay Area Pun-Off has sprung up in

California, and the man who started it is a counselor at a summer camp for adults. Case closed.

Although immaturity is not a 100 percent flattering diagnosis, at least it doesn't equate adult affinity for puns with having the mental faculties of a stroke victim.

At this point, Dr. Hempelmann is just looking at his phone. A couple of conference goers start to file in and gravitate, sleepy-eyed, toward the coffee. I ask if there's anything either of the professors can think of that would help me deliver puns better in a competitive situation, and they look at each other for a moment as if telepathically deliberating over who has to answer me.

"Monosyllables," Dr. Attardo says, finally. "The shorter the word, the easier it is to make a pun because you have a better chance of finding something that's similar to it."

According to Jerzy, longer words are the money words. When I've been practicing, I've racked my brain for these polysyllabic monsters first. But when speed and volume count, maybe there's something to coming up with a few smaller puns to pad out your set. I think back to Jerzy's puns and realize he does that, too. It seems he's just as good at puns as he is at *lying*.

"Also, try not to telegraph the punch line. The more unexpected it is, the greater the level of what we call logical mechanism or justification," Attardo adds. "And if you can, bring in sex. That always gets a reaction."

A Ph.D. student with a serrated buzz cut and combat boots walks in and rubs her hands together. Her name is Elisa and she is ready to give me and some of the other conference goers a tour of the humor lab. It's time to wrap up this conversation. As I'm packing my bag, I ask rather desperately if either of the linguists has any final thoughts about what makes someone proficient at puns.

"I think it's a sign of wit if you can feel language as it happens like muscles moving as you walk," Hempelmann says. "But it could also just be a mental affliction."

It's beginning to feel suspiciously like everybody who knows about puns and brains thinks people who pun a lot have something wrong with their brains. The ability to pun, though, seems to me more like a sign that something is very much right with your brain—as long as you know not to do it, like, during a murder trial. Punning is something the human brain can do but animals and robots cannot. When the inevitable machine uprising and/or *Planet of the Apes* scenario occurs, at least we'll be the only ones able to make puns about it. Even the supercomputer that beat Ken Jennings on *Jeopardy!*, Watson, wasn't able to create wordplay. No computer program has yet replicated what happens in the human brain when a person puns. But I know someone who tried his best to make one.

I first met Max Parke at the Gwiazdowski brothers' podcast recording, and later had lunch with him to talk about his experiment: the Punerator.

Max is a software engineer who has been going to Punderdome for almost four years. He considers himself a jobber, sort of a Washington General of pun competitions whose presence makes the other guys look good. While many competitors each month are actors, comedians, and writers—people who are used to having an audience—Max is a computer programmer, and Punderdome is his lone outlet for performing. About a year into going every month, he decided to combine his career skills with his hobby.

One of the rules of all pun competitions is No Electronic

Assistance. Smartphones are verboten. Max started to wonder, though, exactly what electronic assistance even had to offer. It's not as if you could just whip out your phone when nobody was looking, google "Saturday Morning Cartoon puns" and find several megabytes worth of killer material. Max decided he wanted to test his software skills by creating a computer program that could actually make puns.

His experiment basically followed the logic of Dr. Attardo's Christmas light analogy. Max uploaded an encyclopedic depository of synonyms, antonyms, homonyms, and common phrases associated with a wide range of categories (a string of red lights), along with a rhyming dictionary (a string of white ones). Max's goal was for the Punerator to cross these light-strings automatically and transform relevant words into punny phrases. He was never able to get it to work, mostly for the same reasons English speakers have an advantage over every other culture that puns—which is pretty much all of them.

As I found out from Dr. Lederer, English is uncontestably the best language to pun in. It has by far the largest vocabulary in history, having surpassed a million words in 2009—twice as many words as the second-place Germans. Punning in English is also easier because our vocabulary has absorbed elements of at least three hundred other languages, allowing for puns like "Paris is a *site* for *soirees*." Another reason it's great for punning is it's not an inflected language like Latin or Greek, where certain parts of speech are frozen in carbonite. That blind carpenter who picked up his hammer and *saw*? He is what happens when a noun is transformed into a verb, which in some other languages is simply not possible. Especially, it seems, the language of computers.

The sheer volume of words in any representative corpus

would make too large a search space for a functional algorithm. In order for the Punerator to work, it would also have to go beyond monosyllables and find words that could combine to make up larger words in phrases. Harder still, it would have to do the opposite of disambiguating—an already difficult process for any computer program—in order to turn verbs into nouns, or to use, say, *bank* in a different way than it's intended. The brain can do all these things instantaneously—pull, prod, and recontextualize words—while even the most advanced computer in the world with the most state-of-the-art AI still struggles to replicate such contortions.

Max was never able to get the Punerator to reverse engineer his test case pun: "*Iran* so far away." After he got a job in 2013, at a very popular software company whose name you know well, he gave up on the project and went back to analog punning. Despite the experiment's failure, he remains a far better software engineer than a punner.

The marquee experiment in the humor lab at Texas A&M University-Commerce is at least as ambitious as Max's Punerator. It's an eye-tracking device that reveals how the presence of humor affects smile intensity. The lab is housed inside a redbrick building with the vaguely Epcot-ish title, "Hall of Languages." The layout of the experiment itself reminds me of Peter Venkman's experiments in *Ghostbusters*, but that probably has more to do with the fact that I've observed very few academic experiments outside of a cinematic setting. The eye tracker looks kind of like two baby WALL-E's on an even seesaw. Two strangers sit on opposite sides of a desk with the eye tracker between them. The WALL-E pointing at either person films their faces from an unflattering angle condusive to bullfrog-neck, and sends them to a split-screen display, where their every eye movement is noted. Elisa, the Ph.D. candidate, feeds the two students a script for telling a joke, just to break the ice, and then waits for them to start saying humorous things on their own. When they do, the eye tracker monitors the intensity of smile-change on a scale of one to four.

Elisa tells students she's studying conversation. They have no idea they're actually humor research guinea pigs.

While we're in the lab, one of the conference attendees asks Elisa whether there is any information in the literature about gender or other demographics.

"This *is* the literature," she responds.

Elisa is reevaluating the relationship between smile and laughter and humor in natural conversation, which means there is very little I can extrapolate here that would relate to connecting with a crowd. Although the experiment is far from over, so far it looks like laughter and smiling do not co-occur reliably with punch lines. There could be a bunch of complex neurological reasons for why that is, but what seems more likely is that different people process humor in different ways. The experiment has also revealed rather conclusively, though, what kindergarten teachers have been saying for ages: smiling intensity is contagious. (They may not have used those precise words.) Maybe the key to landing puns is smiling more intensely onstage—even if it sounds like something that will make everybody really uncomfortable if they're not smiling already.

I LAST THROUGH five more interminable sessions with a vast array of PowerPoint styles, before finally fleeing the conference during a coffee break. Before I make my getaway, Dr. Hempelmann pulls me aside and invites me out to the bar where everyone is meeting up later. I'm a little surprised, but I accept.

When you go to a humor research conference, there is inevitably a moment where you stand around at a bar with heavily buzzed academics comparing iPhone podcast apps as if they were résumés. Forget about the string of letters in your official title; these are your real comedy credentials. It's the modern equivalent of giving someone a tour of your bookcase or your music collection, which for a lot of people is done via iPhone now anyway. It's also the first moment I've found common ground with anyone all weekend.

Maybe it's the difference between interviewing first thing in the morning on a Saturday and talking over a beer on Saturday night, postconference, or maybe it's the fact that I've now earned my comedy nerd wings from our podcast comparison, but Hempelmann and I are finally talking about something helpful.

"The way to distinguish a good from a bad pun," he says, cradling a beer stein, "is that it has to fully swing both ways. It cannot just be that you set up one context and then, boom, you go another way with the second sense. That other sense should already have been there."

He cites, as an example, the mad magician that pulled out his *hare*. The only way to improve this pun, he claims, is by hinting at the rabbit, like "The magician had too many animal props so he got mad and pulled out his hare." This doesn't strike me as any improvement, though, because rabbits are for some reason still parasitically inseparable from magicians in this, the second decade of the twenty-first century. But he's absolutely right. Puns need a second sense to work in everyday life—that eureka moment where whatever you've been talking about dovetails with some concurrent element in one perfect word or phrase. But that can't happen at Punderdome.

"In a pun competition, you have to invent the second sense," I point out. "That's why setups always sound so random."

I search the room for an example.

"Like, right now, I can look at this napkin and think, 'Okay, something I sleep with is my *nap-kin*,' but it's not funny because we weren't talking about a thing I sleep with and also looking at this."

"Yeah, it's not funny," Hempelmann says, a little too emphatically. "Maybe make it a little better? Like, 'I had to bunk with my sister and I hadn't done that since we were children: we were *nap-kins.*'"

One of my shoes is tapping extra hard beneath the table. Hempelmann is smiling a little. Are we in a pun-off right now? I race through ideas. *Napkindergarten? Snapkin. Gnat-kin.* I've got nothing. Shit.

"I'm not sure I'm making it better," he says a moment later. "I'm not a comedian."

Just like that, our near pun-off has reached armistice.

"Anyway, it's hard to neatly sneak in two meanings when you're making up a pun off one word," I say, after a while.

"Well, that's exactly what a bad pun is, though. There's a word with punning potential, but then you just force that second sense."

This is, indeed, the third kind of Bad Pun—the kind with a clunky, awkward construction that doesn't quite hold steadily. It's a stretch where reach exceeds grasp, like a punster with his arm extended for a high five that never comes. I search around for a way to make a pun that doesn't fit this description.

"I could say, 'Let's table this for now,' I announce, "and that's almost funny."

"Eh."

"Because we're at a table."

"It is contextually present."

"But it still doesn't quite work," I add, kind of defeated. At this moment, my beer is empty, I've been listening to and talking about humor and puns for forty-eight hours, and I never really found out what accounts for someone like Ben Ziek and his preternatural pun prowess. My brain is starving for pretty much anything except puns right now.

"Yeah, we weren't talking about tables," he says, and I have no response—in pun-form or otherwise.

Fine, I surrender. A great pun, as they say, is its own *reword*. A mediocre pun, though, is just *awkword*.

# 6

## GAMES AND SHOWS

It's only February, but Ben Ziek's year is off to a strong start.

Even though his presence at O. Henry has become as reliable as weather puns in local news, I still ring him up to see if he plans on going this year. It's been a couple months since we last spoke, and perhaps something has come up. Maybe there's an intergalactic pun-off in May, and Ziek has been recruited to defend Earth like in *Space Jam*. Sadly, that is not the case. (Yet!) But just as the sun rises in the east, the planet's reigning champ will return to Austin in a few months to defend his title. At the moment, though, he's excited because he recently passed the online *Jeopardy!* test. He could get a callback any day.

When I check in with each of the Brooklyn crew to see how they're weathering Punderdome's off-season, and to do an O. Henry roll call, it seems like it's been a strong year so far for them as well.

Obviously, both Gwiazdowskis are up for the O. Henry. Jerzy is in Norway through most of February, developing plays with an eager batch of writers, and Jordan is working marathon hours in Queens, overseeing the launch of a hip-hop-themed burger joint. I'm surprised to learn, however, that there's a third brother, Toby, who plans on flying in from Milwaukee to compete for the first time. It appears as though the Pun-Off is going to consist of roughly 7 percent Gwiazdowskis.

Rekho does not plan on attending. She just joined Upright Citizens Brigade's improv touring company, plus she's already been to the O. Henry twice. Isaac is in the middle of directing the first two plays in an ongoing cycle, but he says he's down. So is Sam, who is now rehearsing with a theater company to perform a piece she says is a mashup of Alfred Hitchcock and Eugene Ionesco, something I can't even begin to fathom. Tim has newly left his job writing for the *New York Post* to edit the local focus blog Brokelyn, and he confirms that this is the year he'll finally go to the Pun-Off. Ally is on a family vacation in the Virgin Islands, but she says she's definitely on board. She also says that Nikolai, who beat her in the last Dome back in December and who is currently writing a screenplay in a California cabin, will also be coming along. When we get to Austin, we're going to be rolling heavy. A swarm of Brooklynites is set to descend upon the southern-fried pun convention, like locusts in a triangle offense, and possibly wrest a horse's ass–shaped trophy from Ziek's cobra clutch.

But Ziek isn't thinking about the O. Henry now. He's thinking about *Jeopardy!* Although he's appeared on five TV game shows before, *Jeopardy!* is his white whale. He watches the show religiously and he's tried out for it several times, including once in college. (Interestingly, *Washington Post* columnist and punster Alexandra Petri, who has bested Ziek in Punniest of Show but never Punslingers, did appear on the show as a freshman at Harvard.) Until now, though, he had never passed the initial test, which means he is closer to the dream than ever before.

Ziek's devotion to game shows may seem like a hobby or a quirk at first, but it's more than that. Game shows are his life and livelihood. When he moved to California over a decade ago, it was to pursue a lifelong goal of breaking into the field, both as a contestant and on the production side. He lives in a three-bedroom apartment with four roommates—don't ask about the sleeping arrangements—with whom he runs a side business. Ziek's day job, which he works at night, is at the Burbank Marriott, but he's also a founding partner in Home Game Enterprizes. It's a company that brings the game-show experience directly to corporate seminars and trivia junkies who have very specific ideas about how to party. Imagine *The Price Is Right* on wheels and you're there. A video on the company's website reveals a TED Talk–headsetted Ziek rising from behind a podium like a genie and strutting across the lavender-lit stage in front of a projection of the *Press Your Luck* scoreboard. "Four score," he says in a Lincoln-like timbre, gesturing at the board. We never get to see just how many whammies are forthcoming.

When Ziek and his merry band of Bobs Barker are not putting on game shows for paying customers, they're devouring them at home. Every time a new show rolls out, they analyze and dissect it with clinical detachment to determine which elements are missing. With the recent rise of *Match Game* and *Family Feud,* they're sensing in a licked-finger-in-the-air kind of way a full-blown resurgence of the prime-time game-show craze that took television by storm in the late '90s, just before the onset of the reality TV pandemic. Perhaps there'll soon come a day when Home Game Enterprizes morphs from *The*

*Price Is Right* on wheels into the next *Price Is Right*. Or at least, that's the dream.

Because Ziek hopes to transition into the production area of game shows, he doesn't try out for them much anymore. Potential contestants are immediately disqualified from appearing on shows if they know anybody on staff, and Ziek knows somebody at pretty much every game in town. Some of the other roommates are among this coterie of contacts, having managed to secure jobs at game shows in recent years. *Jeopardy!* is one of the few options still open for Ziek to audition on. He is currently twitchy with callback anticipation now that he's finally passed the test. Game shows are his world and pun competitions are merely a small subsection within that world.

It just so happens that the kind of trivia knowledge that kills on *Jeopardy!* is also what's required to rule Punslingers, even more so than punning. If the category is Beer, it's not enough to say "Your friend is smart, but my *bud's wiser*" or "Overnight success usually takes fifteen *beers*." You have to dig in with the omnidirectional breadth of knowledge to produce brands, brewers, ingredients, varietals, glassware, aspects of the fermentation process, and perhaps even alcohol-related illnesses and paths to recovery. You have to be ready to field questions on the American Civil War and every other topic that Gary Hallock, David Gugenheim, and Brian Oakley have cooked up in the pun lab. You have to be Ken Jennings, essentially, but like if Ken Jennings were also Carrot Top.

O. Henry isn't the only pun competition that resembles a game show, though. Punderdome also has some strains in its DNA. Fred Firestone has always been a game-show obsessive, but in a different way than Ben Ziek. Instead of the trivia aspect, he admired the banter between host and guests, and the general pizzazz of it all. When he was raising Jo Firestone, Fred kept a makeshift set in the garage, where he'd often stage game shows, sometimes involving a ventriloquist dummy and a fake squirrel. Many years later, when they were putting together the Punderdome concept, it was Fred's idea to include the human clap-o-meter—a nod to the *Mad Men*–era game show *Queen for a Day*. And before the duo started having audience members sing sitcom theme songs while the puntestants write their puns down, they originally played the *Jeopardy!* theme.

Because game literally recognize game, when *America's Got Talent* was holding open auditions in New York, producers from the show approached the Firestones. Word about Punderdome had reached the show's representatives, who thought there might be a place for puns in the upcoming tenth season. They asked Jo and Fred to send the most recent winners in for a tryout, which is how Forest Wittyker and Punky Brewster ended up in a warehouse on the far west side of Manhattan one day in fall 2014, auditioning for *America's Got Talent*.

Tim and Rekha cautiously approached Pier 94, which was disconcertingly close to Larry Flynt's Hustler Club. The two friends strode past a squadron of dancers in sequin jumpsuits, an elderly puppeteer, several small children fiddling with bow ties, and a steel drum band playing "Hot Hot Hot" along the way. Eventually, after much filling out of forms, they made it into the austere audition space. Standing between them and their shot at getting on TV sat a matronly woman at a long folding table, a mysterious earpiece jutting out of one ear.

When the woman asked what their talent was, Rekha simply said, "Puns."

"Okay," she replied. "Go!"

Tim did his best to briefly explain how Punderdome works,

and the gatekeeper seemed to get it. She distributed pens and paper and offered up as a topic Fast-Food Restaurants. Rekha and Tim gingerly began scribbling away for the usual ninety seconds. After they were done, the woman noted aloud that in no way would ninety seconds of dead air fly on the show. Her observation proved Fred and Jo prescient for getting audience members to lead *DuckTales* theme song sing-alongs during this downtime. With this preamble out of the way, the woman let Tim and Rekha do their thing.

"Porta-potties with pizza are called *Pop-up Johns*," Rekha said.

"I heard the doors on those porta-potties, you have to jiggle them," Tim shot back. "You have to *Jimmy Johns* open."

Though she never actually laughed, the Cerberus of *America's Got Talent* found this pun duel amusing. She didn't think it was TV-worthy in its current state, but she sensed something there. Since Rekha had been to O. Henry before, she recited her sandwich-based Punniest of Show routine as an example of a prepared bit. The woman was further impressed. She asked the two to make a video performing a new routine as a duo and submit it to the producer who'd initially reached out. Rekha and Tim agreed and left happy, walking past the handlers of a giant Chinese dragon on the way back to the mainland.

Although they were intrigued at first, the idea of competing on TV shed its appeal the more they thought about it. The frenetic alchemy that occurs within Littlefield's walls could never translate to a studio audience that big, they realized, let alone the greater community of Nick Cannon fans watching from home. After a long debate, Tim and Rekha decided not to submit a video.

Had the opportunity fallen to Words Nightmare, though,

she surely would have gone through with it. Ally is the only Punderdome champ anywhere near as obsessed with game shows as Ben Ziek. Her father tried for decades to get on *Jeopardy!*, but never made it. Since then Ally and her brother have attemped to make their father's dreams come true vicariously by trying out for *Jeopardy!* whenever possible. Last summer, Ally finally passed online. She was invited out to Boston for an interview and a separate in-person test. Ally went through with it, but she left Boston with the queasy feeling that neither test nor interview had gone well. She hasn't heard back yet.

A game-show fixation isn't the only thing Ally shares with Ziek, though. She is also well versed in the other major talent that led him to victory so many times at O. Henry: improv.

A GROUP OF people walks onstage, probably wearing a lot of plaid. They have nothing prepared. Somebody tosses out a prompt and then the group has to create something with it that will make strangers laugh. This description could easily apply to either a pun competition or an improv show, also possibly just a scheduling disaster on the part of an overtaxed booker.

It's not a coincidence that every O. Henry champion of the past decade has improv in their background. And not just because improv teams always seem to be named something like *Gonorrhea Perlman* or *I Fart Huckabees*. Punning uses a lot of the same skills as improv, and both are forms of humor that a lot of people think they despise, but actually only do when it's really bad.

When improv goes well, there's nothing like it. A series of spontaneous, twisted theater pieces materialize seamlessly, with no evidence of how they came together. The tone flips on a dime, and the performers make it feel like it was headed that way all along. The dialogue zings like something out of a movie, probably because a lot of movies now aim for an improvised feel. Improv done right is such an impressive feat, schools like The Groundlings and Second City consistently surface future stars like Amy Poehler, Tina Fey, and Key and Peele, who then use those skills to conquer the world.

When improv goes not so well, though, there's also nothing like it. At least bad puns are finished the instant they start. Bad puns rarely spend minutes siphoning off a reservoir of patience before collapsing into a chasm of wacky chairwork. Bad puns spoil conversations, sure, but a bad improv scene will ruin your day and end friendships.

It's partly because of how painful a bad improv scene can be for all involved, though, that performers come into their careers coated with comedy Teflon. Before an improviser's instincts lead him or her anywhere funny, they'll first lead them into a sarlacc pit of stupidity again and again. And that's if the training goes well. Failing miserably a bunch of times is the first step toward mastery. A lot of amazing scenes come from a performer's willingness to risk things going terribly. By the time an improviser has any sort of grip on what he or she is doing, they will have endured failure so many times it has less impact than a cloudy day. The part of them that's afraid of messing up or looking stupid simply gets burned off like leftover gunk in a self-cleaning oven. After thirteen years of performing improv, for instance, Ben Ziek's fear-oven is sparkly clean.

Because my own personal oven is disgusting, though, as if a vat of fully loaded buffalo nachos exploded inside and was left unattended for weeks, I sign up for a one-off class at People's Improv Theater to see what improv failure really feels like.

Turns out it feels like extreme discomfort and embarrassment.

The very first thing we do is stomp around in a circle on the hardwood floor like we're protesting the size of the room. Our unruly group forms less a circle than a small child's drawing of a circle, with fat smudge lines. We're told to look fully into one another's eyes, which everybody is now doing with sunny, hypercaffeinated smiles. It's been less than three minutes and I'm already in over my head. The indoor march of the penguins soon evolves when the instructor asks us to chase each other around, the sound of our shuffling footsteps occasionally punctuated with racquetball squeaks. Anyone viewing through the window would assume we were playing a kindergarten recess game invented by other kindergartners.

Later, we're urged to partner up with someone and stare into that person's eyes. I turn toward the straw-haired ex-biker lady standing next to me and we mutually shrug. I take a deep breath, settle into what I hope is a neutral but game expression, and peer into her soul. The intensity of this exercise instantly melts my brain into a meat-puddle. If I was in over my head before, I am now dead and buried. I start thinking irrational thoughts like *She knows!* and try to force my vision to go blurry. My partner clears her throat without moving her face, like a ventriloquist, and I want to run out of the room screaming bloody murder.

All is silent except for the instructor's voice, which is soft like a guided meditation.

"Do nothing," he says. "Each time you worry you should be doing something, do even less."

I now know my stare partner's eye color in more elaborate detail than my wife's. Someone adjusts posture slightly, and a floorboard creaks. I think: *Don't move.* Every now and then, a burst of shouting wafts in from some other room, cutting the quiet, and I can only imagine what's going on in there.

"Look at this person across from you and know that at some point today, they either have pooped or will poop."

The face across from me convulses into a smile that screams "Yep!" Her joy is conspiratorial. She's looking at me like I maybe poop more than the average person, either in amount or frequency. I so want this to be over.

When the exercise does end, it's as if we're released from an enchantment, unstuck in time. We had been staring at each other's faces for five minutes and twenty-seven seconds, which is at least five minutes longer than I'd ever stared into someone's face before or since.

Later, we actually do improvise some scenes and I get the full thrust of what improv failure feels like. When I trade terms of endearment with a British Ira Glass look-alike in front of class that day, it is to dead silence. A total void. A black hole of antilaughter. It feels like I just got turned down for a marriage proposal, and continuing on with the scene afterward feels like asking the nearest bystander to marry me instead. Suddenly I realize just how much I've been graded on a curve at Punderdome. It's such a supportive crowd, with such a specific sensibility, that most of the time, as long as you make any sort of effort at a joke, you get a bubble cushion of polite laughter. Here, there were no guarantees other than a guarantee that you would *not* get a laugh unless you did something amazing, and the key to figuring out how to do that involved completely laughless vacuums like this one. I can scarcely imagine how anyone could continue doing this until they master it.

Ben Ziek has stuck with it since 1998, when he tried starting an improv group as a college student in Kutztown, Pennsylvania. The group went on to perform one show together, which a local paper wrote up—mainly because one of the members had gotten a perfect score on his SATs and there was apparently no news about Monica Lewinsky that day. Eventually, Ziek moved to California and began taking classes at Comedy Sportz, the organization whose name best describes what pun competitions are. Although he never joined one of the house teams of pro performers there, Ziek worked for a long time on the Rec League, which puts on Monday night shows for free. Years later, while doing a show with a theater called the LA Connection, for a private school in Studio City, he performed alongside LL Cool J. Although the star of *NCIS: Los Angeles* didn't do much improv himself, when he approved of something Ziek did, he made him turn it into a song. Jamming out for Ladies Love is one of Ziek's fondest professional memories. He may have gotten the most mileage out of his improv skills so far, though, on the O. Henry stage.

One of the central tenets of improvisation is "Yes-and." It's the idea of agreeing with your scene partner and building off whatever they've just said. When Ziek squares off against an opponent in Punslingers, his ears are wide open and his antennae are tingling. All that training in letting one idea trigger another has taught him to listen reflexively and return fire rapidly. It's also taught him to observe more. In addition to listening onstage, sometimes Ziek will look out into the crowd and scan the surroundings. If he has a moment while his opponent is sweating out a pun, Ziek will search the nearby buildings, the food vendors, the trees, the lawn-chair-bound spectators—looking for anything he can build into a pun. No matter what the topic, there's bound to be visual material out there somewhere—and improvisers know how to use the whole buffalo.

Of course, Ziek wasn't the first improviser to make the pilgrimage to pun mecca. When I visited Austin, I kept hearing about the improv scene's impact on the O. Henry over the past decade, and Valerie Ward was often cited as Patient Zero.

Valerie is an improv performer and teacher at Austin's Hideout Theater, the owner of a vegan ice cream shop, and a former champion and judge at the O. Henry. She first discovered pun competitions as a college student in 2004, at a point when she'd already been doing improv for years. Although she went home empty-handed her first competition, she had so much fun she decided to make a tradition of going every year. The next time, she nearly beat David Gugenheim, who now runs the O. Henry, in a half-hour nail-biter that clinched her an MVP Award.

Gugenheim couldn't have known it at the time, but it was the end of an era.

"I went up at O. Henry, then a few other improvisers did it independently," Valerie says, showing me around the Hideout Theater. Her floral headscarf kind of matches the colorful triptych of canvases suspended by wires above the stage, which together form an apocalyptic sky.

"It felt for a long time like the Pun-Off was a local thing, something just for . . . the old group," she says, eyes wide like she has scorching gossip about mutual friends. "Then, more recently, it started getting injected with newer, younger people from around the country—improv people and slam poets."

Some of these new people arrived in Austin unexpectedly, under less than ideal circumstances. In the wake of Hurricane Katrina, a group of displaced New Orleanians sought refuge in Austin while assessing the damage to their homes. Arthur

Simone was among their number, part of a group of improvisers who ran a theater together back in New Orleans. Despite their dismal situation, or perhaps because of it, they spent this purgatorial time in Austin exploring the city's thriving improv community. When their houses ultimately proved damaged beyond repair, they decided to stick around and set up shop. A pair of local business owners let Simone and the others from New Orleans use the back of their video store as a performance arts space for a couple months, rent-free. It was here that the group founded ColdTowne Theater, on a budget of $500 and with only six students. They then went on to open their own space and further grow the theater. Their success energized an already flourishing scene and eventually spun off a second theater called the New Movement. Simone also joined Valerie Ward as one of the first improvisers to participate in the O. Henry, along with Matt Pollock, a computer programmer who also performed improv at the Hideout.

The punning community in Austin is similar to the one in Brooklyn. Everyone is interested in hanging out and growing creatively and being fans of one another, rather than the competitive aspect. Even though they were from different theaters, Arthur, Valerie, and Matt would stage informal pun-offs with another local improviser, Dav Wallace, to get ready for the real thing. In the years following the competitive retirement of David Gugenheim and Brian Oakley, one improviser or another has won Punslingers every single year, whether it was an Austinite or Ben Ziek. (Wallace and Pollock are the only people who have been able to defeat Ziek at Punslingers yet.)

Another way improv factors into pun competitions is that it helps players always keep a couple rounds in the chamber. The way some performers approach a scene is to unpack the setting

like they're sifting through a dossier. If the scene is set in a coffee shop, for instance, they'll do a mental inventory of all the
things that would be inside a coffee shop—studious laptoppers,
a breakup in progress, a screeching grinder, a vegan exasper-
ated by the lack of almond milk—and store that data until they
need it. Being able to stack and index information in your mind
is like a cheat code for pun competitions. The cue words are
floating at the top of your brain, waiting for you to pluck them
out and deploy them at will.

Even without a bunch of puns at the ready, though, a seasoned improviser can stare into the gaping maw of a waiting
crowd, and elegantly spin their wheels. Sometimes improv just
amounts to doing trust fall challenges with your mind.

"The MCs at Punslingers seemed to get a little annoyed with
us at first because you have to start talking within a certain
amount of time and come to your pun," Valerie says. "I think
everyone mostly had these little one-liners before, but if you get
an improviser up there, they'll be, like, 'Well, I can just start
talking and I don't know what I'm gonna say but I'll get there.'"

They've continued taking their time getting there since.

Matt Pollock recently became a father and has since lapsed
in his improv and punning duties. Arthur and Valerie are both
skipping the O. Henry in May as well. But Ben Ziek and Dav
Wallace will be there, and so will Punderdomers like the Gwiazdowskis and Nikolai and Sam and Isaac, who all have improv
experience as well. (Tim Donnelly stands out as being one of
the few Punderdome champs to have never "taken a suggestion
from the audience.") There is no reason to suspect the streak of
improviser wins won't continue.

Although plenty of people like Matt Pollock have arrived

at punning through improv, there are also people like Words Nightmare who did the opposite.

When Ally first went to Punderdome, years ago, it was on a date with her then boyfriend. She was in something of a spiritual free fall at the time, having just graduated from a master's program in ergonomic engineering, without being certain it was what she wanted to do with her life. One day, her boyfriend suggested they compete at Punderdome, which they did under the name Punning Linguists. Their category was American Comfort Foods, and each approached it from angles that were uncomfortable in different ways. Ally joked about wanting her boyfriend to propose ("If he wants to maintain the *peas,* he best get me some *carats*") and he joked about a very strange sex act ("How about *spaghet-these balls-on-nas*al?")

They did not make it to the next round, or the next stage of their relationship. Ally eventually came back as a solo act, though, and won. The Punderdome experience had a profound effect on her, beyond the thrill of victory. She felt a kinship with people so unapologetically into a very specific thing necessarily embraced by the masses. It was like finding an overlooked pocket of civilization that spoke her language. What really surprised her was how much she enjoyed getting up in front of a crowd—the fizzy euphoria of the unfolding moment. It made her reconsider everything.

"I realized maybe all this time I've been thinking I want to be a designer because it allows me to be creative in a way where other people are able to appreciate what I've made," Ally says one day over coffee. "But maybe it doesn't have to be *things* I make, but ideas or conversations. So I started doing a lot of evaluating about what I wanted to actually be doing."

Ally quit her job at Warby Parker and began working free-lance. Around the same time, she attended a friend's show at the People's Improv Theater in Manhattan and became enam-ored with the place. Another friend was interning at PIT in ex-change for improv class credits, an ideal option for Ally's new freelance budget. She worked out a similar arrangement and is currently on track to finish the fifth and final level at PIT soon after the next Punderdome in March.

It did not take many classes for Ally to notice that her im-prov training funneled directly into her punning efforts.

Because she's a fellow *Jeopardy!* nerd like Ziek, Ally has an endless well of references to draw upon for puns. Improv trained her to quickly mine the furthest regions of her brain for Punderdome gold. It was partly just getting used to react-ing in the moment, but there was something beyond Pavlovian improv response. Along with yes-and, another central tenet of the form is finding the less obvious way to approach anything. That kind of lateral thinking is exactly what helps Ziek turn his trivia knowledge into puns. Sometimes Ally would get a cate-gory she knew nothing about, and rather than dig deep for info embedded in her subconscious, she would look for the loop-hole. If she didn't know baseball, maybe she knew some base-ball movies and team names. When a category like Sources of Light came her way, she knew she could use anything naturally bright, units of light measurement, shiny appliances, whatever. There was always a way.

Outside of improv and punning, Ally explored other cre-ative outlets, going to open mics to try her hand at stand-up, and writing the odd piece for the female-centric satirical site Reductress. She bonded with her fellow Dome champion Sam, and the two began putting on a monthly comedy show, and eventually became roommates. Her entire life had become one big yes-and, agreeing with the possibilities that came her way and building off them.

While Ally has only done more and more improv since she started punning, Ben Ziek has done less. A couple of years after he first competed in O. Henry, he stopped altogether. On the surface, the reason is because this was around the time he began his new sideline in wrestling, as both a manager and the occasional performer Lex Icon. With all the time he now spent training wrestlers and himself, he didn't have enough time to keep up the weekly shows. Perhaps, though, there was another reason he'd stopped doing improv. With the O. Henry Pun-Off, Ziek had finally found the perfect synthesis of his two hobbies—improv and game shows—and had no use for the former on its own anymore. Although the two interests can work together nicely, they're also in direct conflict with each other: one is just for fun, and the other is something that can be won.

# 7

## ALL THE PUNS THAT ARE FIT TO PRINT

The dawn of spring is upon us. Meteorologically speaking, it's still very much winter, with air-conditioning units across Brooklyn serving as dust farms for at least ten more weeks, but tonight Punderdome returns from its respite.

Over the past couple months, I've had several Richard Linklater films' worth of dialogue about competitive punning. What I haven't done, though, is actually competed. Walking down Fourth Avenue against the wind, swathed in a hoodie and puffy jacket, I feel cautiously optimistic. I'm bracing for that same naked-at-school feeling as before, only I've practiced enough since last year to have reasonable expectations by now. It feels like a test. A referendum. Maybe I'll do so well that the audience goes into pep rally hysterics and Little Debbie Zebra Cakes rain from the sky. But maybe not!

Once inside Littlefield, I neatly scrawl "Punter S. Thompson" on a name tag and slap it on my chest. A steady torrent of shivering bodies trudges in after me, scanning for places to stash their jackets and bags instead of using coat check. Pretty soon, the house is packed. A sizable chunk of the crowd is set in reunion mode, all bear hugs and head nods, and a few familiar faces are floating above name tags. Isaac, a.k.a. Punder Enlightening, is off to the side, near the DJ booth, and I go over to ask him about the play cycle he directed last month. A smiling dude with a shaved head and narrow, close-set features sidles up to us with a name tag clasped in his hand and asks about how Punderdome works. He knew enough to get here early, apparently, but he has no idea what happens now.

As the warm-up begins, Tim flags me down. It's the first time we've seen each other in months, and his ginger beard has grown several centimeters in the winter chill. He looks like he came straight from a double makeup shift at the co-op, which is not something I know him to do but would not be surprised if he did. We hang out near the bar, waiting for his girlfriend, Meghan, with whom he's just moved in. It's also the first time I've seen Tim since he left his job writing for the *New York Post*.

"What was it like working there, anyway?" I ask. "Was it just puns all day?"

"You have no idea."

Before we can delve into the subject any deeper, Jo starts calling out the first round of names. One of them is Punter S. Thompson. Tim smiles and claps me on the back and I get moving. I push through the crowd like a gentle Godzilla, careful not to stomp over the purses and tote bags on the floor, hopeful that people see my name tag and panic-eyes and know I'm not doing this merely to get in prime spectating position.

Once onstage, everybody arranges themselves in writing poses, either kneeling on the floor or hunched over the edge of the plastic picnic table behind us, like we simultaneously all lost contact lenses. The category is . . . Plants.

A laser light show of vegetation unspools in my brain, an undulating abundance of leafy greens and foliage. I need words, though. Sound over meaning. As a woman in a Wilma Flintstone–esque white dress sings *The Fresh Prince of Bel-Air* theme song, words invade my mind like a fleet of tiny ninjas. Syllables divide. Tulips becomes *two lips*. Orchid becomes *or kid*. Bigger words appear, too—big, juicy, multisyllabic language husks with hidden innards waiting to emerge. Chlorophyll, that's something. Photosynthesis? Chrysanthemum? I can work with those. What else? *What else?*

"Markers down!" Jo yells. "Hand 'em over."

I look at my half-empty board like it's a traitor. There are only six words, only two of those words are puns, and both are Bad. The naked hallway moment is about to be a reality. But the worst that could happen suddenly doesn't seem so bad.

Fred turns around and scans the row of punsters. His eyes land on Punder Enlightening.

Isaac walks forward to a generous helping of cheers and puts a hand to his cheek like an aw-shucks debutante.

"Wow, usually I don't get that much applause," he says. "Must be a couple *plants* out there."

A ripple of jolly, eager laughter roils through the crowd. Punderdome is now truly back.

Isaac's approach is shock and awe—a barrage of single-word puns with clear, compact setups, sometimes two or three in a sentence, and all with a nuanced delivery. Jordan Gwiazdowski calls Isaac the Used Car Salesman of Puns; if you don't like one, he's got another to apologize for that first one with, and another after that. *What will it take to get you inside this pun?*

When the buzzer goes off, Isaac manages to squeeze out a final entry: "I used to tell people I could grow plants on my foot, but I was lying: It was a *faux-toe synthesis.*"

Before I even have time to process that "photosynthesis" is now off the table, Fred turns around, looks directly at me, and squints to read my name tag. This is it.

I step over to the mic a moment later and try to let my intuitive brain take over. What good did my cognitive brain ever do anyway, besides come up with a handful of terms from Intro to Earth Science? The first thing my intuition does is eighty-six "two lips," since that's just beyond obvious.

"I'm kind of a mechanic with these puns," I start. "I got these *tool-hips* over here."

The crowd applauds as I shake my hips a little, a thing I had not considered might ever happen. Then, without intending to, I go in and out of a narrative about what's happening onstage.

"I don't want to *bore or fill* you with bad puns," I say, and the audience cheers. I make an allusion to Christopher Walken to force a chrysanthemum pun, and miraculously they laugh at that, too. I'm just about done, but there's still the matter of whether to do "photosynthesis." Fuck it.

"I'm a visual thinker so I didn't do that well presenting in college: I put way too many *photos in thesis.*"

Nobody boos or throws whiskey-ice at me for reusing Isaac's cue word. Instead, the cheers that send me off are notably louder than last time. The crowd isn't being polite; I've improved.

Up last is the defending champ, Daft Pun, who used to be part of a duo, but started performing alone while retaining the name, like Axl with Guns N' Roses. Nikolai has a soft, spindly voice with the inflection of a narcotized indie rock Valley girl. He delivers his puns as though they're a sweet surprise to him.

"I have a coat made from the beard hair of a famous actor," he says, scratching his head. "It's a Michael *Douglas fir* coat."

This one gets a huge laugh and the next one does not, which is probably how Nikolai ends up closing out on a run of celebrity names.

"Do you wanna know who's my favorite actor in the plant-based remake of *Mad Men*? Elizabeth *Moss*. Or the plant-based remake of *Twin Peaks*? Lara Flynn *Soil*. Or the plant-based remake of the presidential election? *Fernie* Sanders."

Both he and Isaac advance forward when the clap-o-meter is introduced, and I am just barely edged out by If Looks Could Kale, who has also improved. It's a little disappointing, but I'm still high from having done better than before.

In the next heat, the first-timer who'd asked Isaac and me how Punderdome works earlier—the Pundance Kid, he's called—comes up with several puns, all with decent setups, and gets a lot of laughs. Not bad for a first-timer, or even a second-or third-timer, actually. Words Nightmare follows him and she punctuates her puns with a self-deprecating meta-narrative about how this turn is going. It's a hit. Both of them move on.

In the final heat of the first round, Jerzy and Jordan perform as a team. The pair strides out to the front of the stage, grinning like Siamese cats who very recently shared a Siamese canary. Their category is: Pizza.

"I don't come to Punderdome to meet friends," Jordan says, his voice dropping an octave. "I come to *meat lovers*."

Everybody in the entire audience roars.

"This guy is *s'silly*, isn't he?" Jerzy says, crooking a thumb at his brother. "If you wonder whether punning is genetic, our *ma's-a-real-a* good punner, too."

They each get another few turns in, and Jordan closes out by leading the crowd in a singing chant of John Lennon's "Give *Pizza* Chance." No Las Vegas oddsmaker would take a bet against the Gwiazdowskis making it to the next round.

Finally, it's Tim's turn. He goes high-concept, using only the names of pizza places—mostly New York spots. Tremors of barely contained excitement run through his body as he twitches onstage. All these years in, and he's still nervous.

"I guess there's no *topping* that," he says, closing with a goofy shrug at the audience.

This is Tim's style. He always pushes himself to find some thread of a story to lace through his puns. Unlike Jerzy, Isaac, and many of the other champs, Tim's only performing experience is doing this. He has no improv training. He's never acted. All he has are his wits and his skill as a writer. As he gets voted on to the next round moments later, I'm suddenly more curious about why he wanted to leave the *New York Post*. It's a media outlet unquestionably committed to puns; why wouldn't Tim want to work there? Of course, when wordplay is part of your job, it ultimately becomes wordwork.

BEFORE MAKING PUNS was part of Tim's job description, he had already worked somewhere surrounded by puns all day. The first employer to incorporate Tim's hobby into his career was Trader Joe's. It was there, in 2011, walking through aisles choked with Speculoos Cookie Butter and Sockeye Salmon Fillets, that he first stumbled upon punning as a game.

Trader Joe's is thick with puns. Stroll into any store and you'll be instantly confronted by colorfully chalked signage promising prices that are "un-be-*cheese*-able" and exhorting you to "have a *rice* day." Punning is a nationwide company initiative here, one that Tim and the other cashiers chose to embrace by mimicking. They made up puns about the store's suspiciously low-priced products—*What is the* dill *with these pickles?*—in an attempt to outpun whoever was running this operation.

They played other games, too. When Tim and a friend were ringing up customers side by side, they passed the time by daring each other to work certain words into the store's seemingly inescapable checkout chitchat. The only rule was that they had to slip in the bingo word naturally. If it was *boxcar,* for instance, they couldn't simply solicit opinions on boxcars. That would be cheating. Instead, when Tim was challenged with that word, and his very next customer asked whether he had a trash bin behind the counter, Tim replied: "Of course! We don't live like boxcar hobos back here." The other cashier heard him say it and reacted with a boom-goes-the-dynamite gesture that his customer would've had to be truly checked out not to notice.

After getting wind of Punderdome shortly after Jo Firestone launched it, Tim and another Trader Joe's friend, Noah, were soon figuring out how to wedge words into sentences onstage. Noah punned under the name Black Punther, and became the Dome's first reigning champion—although Tim wasn't far behind, and both ended up facing off against Jerzy a lot in his earliest days. For one night each month, hundreds of people cheered for the kind of goofy puns Tim made at work about gluten lovers being *lack-toast* intolerant. It was his first taste of performing, and he liked it.

As he flourished onstage, though, Tim's writing career also developed. He started submitting pieces to Brokelyn, where he would eventually become an editor, and which led to a trial run writing features at the *Post*. With his command of punny house style and habit of procuring great quotes, Tim was eventually hired on at the only newspaper whose pun headlines have been collected into a book, 2008's *Headless Body in Topless Bar*.

"It's probably the thing that most makes us famous, and the thing that people are most interested in," Margi Conklin, Sunday editor at the *Post*, told me.

Anybody living in New York has felt the *NYP* effect before. It's a phenomenon where something happens in the world and, whatever your politics, you absolutely need to know how the *Post* will approach it in shouty World War III font. You can't wait to get near a newsstand to see. Will it be shockingly blunt, like telling disgraced Subway spokesman Jared Fogle to ENJOY A FOOT LONG IN JAIL? Or just as vitriolic but more compact, like the front page devoted to a steroid-abusing A-Rod that just read A-HOLE? The *New York Daily News* is a distant second for puns and audacity, but the *Post* is the paper whose headlines most regularly inspire headlines *about* those headlines.

The puns aren't restricted to the front page, either. Beyond the "wood," an old media term for the lead headline dating back to the days when they were printed using giant wooden blocks, puns are peppered liberally throughout the entire paper. As Tim soon found out, they weren't just encouraged; they were practically enforced. It's no accident that almost every lede on every story in the news section usually has a pun or two in it.

"All the writers are expected to know how to play with words in the body text, not just headlines," Conklin says. "Some writers take to it more than others, but if you're good with puns, that will probably help with your writing here generally."

One of Tim's first assignments was about discounts on fitness deals for the New Year, and his editor sent the piece back because the writing "wasn't snappy enough." He then revised it, packed in fitness wordplay like "run to the gym" and "sweat these deals," and the story ran. His editor appeared to share some core values with Punderdome.

Because of the paper's reputation, the fake *Post* headline has become a trope in movies and TV shows. Few manage to get it quite right, though. Margi Conklin remembers being appalled by the pilot episode of the Showtime series *Billions*, in which the *Post* devotes a front page to Damian Lewis's character buying a place in the Hamptons using hedge fund profits. The wood reads BEACH BUM. It's sort of close but not quite right, like a clone of you who hates eating and never gets sleepy in the middle of the day. At least when *30 Rock* did a fake *Post* headline, the writers doubled down on ridiculousness. In one episode, the family of Rip Torn's character, Don Geiss, fights for control of his business, somehow resulting in the wood MEMOIRS OF A GEISS-HA! (When Tina Fey's Liz Lemon sees the headline, she adds that she'd have gone with GEISS SCREAMS: SON PAY.)

The reason editors are defensive about the paper's pun headlines is because so much care goes into creating them. The copy desk receives designs for each page with an empty display area, the allotted space dictating how long the headline should run. Unlike at the O. Henry or Punderdome, electronic assistance is not forbidden. The editors use word association sites to spark ideas for common phrases, and the rhyming dictionary site Rhymezone to help twist them into something new. They use IMDb, Wikipedia, and digital thesauruses. But even with so much pun hardware, the editors sometimes still fall back on tried-and-true hacks like Domers do. In the same way the topic of musical instruments may more than once spur Jerzy to say "*guitar* asses in gear," *Post* editors know that in a pinch, a plan for the subway might be "on track" or "derailed," and if the story pertains to education, someone could be a "class act" or have a "teachable moment." They'll find a pun one way or another.

When the copy desk writes most headlines, each of the eight editors works individually. It's a different story when it comes to the wood, though. The front-page headline is by far the one that gets the most attention. Sometimes it takes a village to create, but even then it's considered an honor to be the one who finally nails it. The higher-ups might have an idea already by the time the copyeditors get in at 3:30 A.M.; more often than not, everyone pitches in. The process resembles an overcaffeinated office pun competition as the group brainstorms variations on a theme. The ideas build as they bounce from person to person, like a chaotic game of Telephone, with shouting instead of whispering. The highest-ranking editors may have the final say, but when someone expels the perfect headline, everyone knows it.

Brayden Simms, a copyeditor who competed at the *Post*'s Punderdome event in 2015, remembers his first time pitching the wood. (This is, unfortunately, not the kind of book where the phrase 'pitching the wood' can be uttered without pausing to reflect on it.) Brayden was the new guy on the copy desk the previous year, when Anthony Weiner was considering getting back into politics. The senator's initial sex scandal had ushered in a golden age of headlines, solidifying his status as a godlike deity in the pantheon of puns. (The puntheon, if you will, and I totally understand if you will not.) Weiner was one of the great headline muses in the paper's storied history. If his surname and infamy didn't move you to high art, perhaps you were working at the wrong place. On this occasion, one of Brayden's coworkers suggested WEINER RISES AGAIN, and another kept the Jesus riff going with RES-ERECTION. That's when Brayden connected the dots. He felt a tad too bashful to say this particular idea out loud, so instead he emailed it to his boss. When that editor read the pitch, WEINER'S SECOND COMING, he stood up and started a slow clap. This headline was technical perfection.

"Sometimes it's better to not overthink the pun," says Deb Pines, another copyeditor who competed at the *Post* Punderdome. "You let words tumble through your head that you associate with the story, then a phrase might come to mind and you just fix it."

That was Deb's approach when she nailed the wood on a story about a panicky JetBlue pilot. She'd already ruled out JET-BLUENATIC and was struggling, until she remembered an earlier headline. It was a story about a flight attendant who had been so fed up with the plane's passengers, he quit his job, grabbed a beer, and went down the plane's emergency chute. That story's headline was FREAKING FLYER, which laid the groundwork for Deb's eventual winner, THIS IS YOUR CAPTAIN FREAKING. It's one of her proudest professional moments.

The first time Tim Donnelly was asked to help out on a headline, he felt like he was being called up to the big leagues. He was cultivating a reputation for puns at a place where a talent like that would not go unnoticed. After a year of working for the paper, he wrote a feature about Punderdome and even talked his editor, Margi Conklin, into attending the show. One day, Tim heard Margi and some other editors in the office struggling to come up with the headline for a story. They were pushing the half-hour mark, the unofficial limit for how long is too long to spend on a headline, when a voice very clearly said, "Is Tim out there? Bring Tim in."

The man who sometimes goes by Forest Wittyker cracked his knuckles and walked into the room. He was on hallowed ground. Every time he'd taken the Punderdome stage had been practice for this moment. But coming up with a headline is harder than coming up with a typical pun setup. The pun in a headline has to play off both the sound of the words and the direction of the story. Also, it has to be polished enough to seem obvious in retrospect. The ideal pun headline should make readers furious they didn't come up with it first.

In this case, the story was about a heroin-addled chef who worked at a fancy French restaurant. After a moment of consideration, Tim looked deep within and pulled out: SMACK MY BISQUE UP. It didn't make it into the paper, but it earned a place on the wall of great rejected headlines—not a metaphor, there is a wall—and established an open-door policy for Tim to pitch going forward. While he never came up with the wood in his tenure at the *Post*, Tim spent the rest of his time there helping out with puns as needed. When a bad review of the *Minions* movie required a very short headline, he was there (DUMB "MINION"). When a story about the opening of an international-themed food court at the Brooklyn Flea in Queens lacked a pithy headline, he came through (WORLD'S FARE). As much as he was now a part of the team, though, Tim eventually had to compete against his own colleagues at the *New York Post* Punderdome.

The copyeditors he would be up against, including Brayden Simms and Deb Pines, were not performers—just like Tim himself before he'd started punning. Fred Firestone and Margi Conklin had accounted for this distinction when they teamed up to plan the event. They knew they needed a different way for the editors to compete. The solution was to have them skip the opening rounds and come out in the semifinals to do the wood onstage. A techie projected the *Post* front-page template onto a screen above the stage, like the bat signal, and when punticipants shouted their headlines, they appeared on-screen. That's how Brayden and Deb found themselves doing an essential part of their jobs in front of five hundred people.

The news story Fred picked for the semifinals involved two brothers fighting inside a McDonald's. When the clock started ticking, the two copyeditors went into work mode, racking their brains for the most appropriate pun headline. After ninety seconds, they had three options. Jerzy and Ally had six. The first thing Brayden had thought of was EXTRA ASSAULT. It was only after the buzzer that he came up with what he felt was the Double Quarter Pounder of this round, GOLDEN ARCH NEMESIS. Deb went first for their team, using MAC ATTACK. When it was Ally's turn, though, she did ARCH ENEMY, pulling the pun out from under Brayden. During the middle of his turn, he came up with SCRAPPY MEAL, which got a laugh, but not enough of one to win.

"We were quick, but nowhere near as quick as the Punderdome people," Deb says.

She and Brayden walked away from the event with a new respect for Tim and the friends on whose side he'd competed. They instantly got the appeal that drew him to the Punderdome stage. As copyeditors, they'd both anonymously contributed *Post* headlines that had been covered on TV and talked about in subways, and bars, and office break rooms all over. This was the first time they got credit for a pun headline beyond the newsroom. It was intoxicating. Tim got that feeling every month, though, so when he had another work opportunity, coming up with the wood wasn't enticement enough to stay.

BACK AT LITTLEFIELD for the first Punderdome of the year, I do a whiskey shot with Ally and the Gwiazdowskis between rounds. Now that I'm out of the running, there's no fear that whiskey will short-circuit my brain.

In the first heat of the second round, the category is Celebrities, which should be illegal for the Gwiazdowskis, since they routinely play a celebrity name game on their podcast. Surprisingly, Jordan and Jerzy's turn is kind of a nonstarter. They will be lucky to make it to the next round.

"It's intimidating to be up here," says the Pundance Kid next. "There's a lot of experienced punners here and I'm just the Paul *Newman*."

The thing is, even though it's his first time, he doesn't seem like the Paul Newman. Pundance looks very comfortable on-stage and he's got incredible timing.

"Just trying to keep the *Streep* alive . . . as is her makeup team," he says at one point, waiting just long enough into the audience's mock-outraged laugh to apologize. He knows exactly what he's doing.

When it's Ally's turn, she goes even deeper into Woody Allen territory than before.

"Is this whole self-deprecating thing working? I don't know, time will tell," she says. "If not, I'll just *dust-it Hoff, man*." She sounds almost on the verge of a breakdown, which is in keeping with her stage persona, but some reality may be filtering in, too.

Daft Pun won his earlier turn with a run of celebrity puns, and momentum is still on his side. He gets a huge laugh with an actress who moonlights as a crime boss obsessed with clear wrap: *Susan Saran-don*. Then he keeps going strong.

When the clap-o-meter comes out, Nikolai and Pundance Kid move forward to the semifinals. As everyone leaves the stage, Jerzy and Jordan look like that tense couple at a dinner party who makes other couples tap each other on the leg under the table.

The category closing out the second round is Sports. Ariel is up—as part of a duo called Pundercats, rather than her usual P-Witty solo act. Both Pundercats wear sheepish grins due to their limited sports knowledge, and it works in their favor. Puns like "*Kobe* or not *Kobe* . . . ," charm laughs out of every corner of the room. When Isaac does his turn next, he continues the sports-ignorance trend, and he absolutely destroys.

"To me, a *touchdown* is sampling pillows at Bed Bath & Beyond," he says. "To me, a *free throw* is when I find a small rug on the ground." The response is monstrous.

Tim is batting cleanup, and he goes the conceptual route again. He warns the crowd up front that he's going to mix football and basketball puns.

"I'm going to try to *court* some favor," he says, "and I might be a little *Bull*-ish when mixing these, so stay with me while I *Ram* them down your throat."

The incoming laughs are tepid.

In his green army jacket and gray wool cap, Tim is visibly sweaty. You can practically see him deciding to switch horses midstream and abandon the cross-sports routine.

"Guess you're not with me on the mixing of puns!" he says, jumping up and down as if to shake off the mixed response. When he apologizes if his previous pun was an *offensive line*, though, there's a shift in the crowd. They're back on his side. The next few puns in a row land, too, and there are huge cheers as he walks back to join the others. It isn't enough, though. Pundercats and Isaac move on, leaving Tim in the dust.

That's the difference between a pun here and one in a newspaper. A *New York Post* headline needs to be in service of showing the angle of the article or making a point. Here, though, the most important thing is making the crowd laugh. Period.

A weird thing usually happens in the semifinals at Punderdome. The performers start to look zonked out while the audience gets progressively more hyped. So it's as if everybody knows the strain Nikolai's brain is under when his pun for the category of Countries is one about the German version of the medical soap opera, *Hamburg E.R.*, and it gets a big laugh.

The Pundance Kid is still slick and composed when he rolls out his next set of puns.

"My cousin is a personal *Hero*shima of mine," he says, which is almost empirically unfunny. But then he follows it up with, "That joke might be the worst thing that ever happened to that city," and the crowd cracks up.

Jo mentions at the beginning of every Punderdome that success here is 90 percent how you present your puns, and this guy proves it more than anyone I've seen so far.

When it's Pundercats' turn, Ariel is still going strong but her partner is flagging. Tracey starts out with a weak pun about "That rapper, *Manila* Ice," and follows it up with "You better *Belize* it." They have a hard time getting the crowd back on their side.

Somehow, there is no distinguishing between the energy level of Isaac's third round and his first, though. He makes a joint-holding gesture and says, "Anybody want another *toke, yo*?" and the laughter barely dies down before he follows it up with "Okay, if you don't—does *Tia wanna*?" Everybody onstage is laughing, too, even Ariel's Pundercats partner, Tracey, who looked bummed a moment before. "Oh no, you dropped the bowl," Isaac says, thriving on this weed run. "Where'd the *glass go*?"

The clap-o-meter gives Isaac a 9.5 and not a 10, even though the room is positively heaving with applause for him. Every-body boos the clap-o-meter.

Pundance Kid gets a 9.5 also. He and Isaac will be sparring in the final round together.

We've finally come to the most inherently O. Henry–like moment of Punderdome. This is when the ramshackle, sum-mer camp talent show air intensifies into something more like a rap battle during open mic night at the Laugh Factory—8 *Mile* for people more likely to listen to a Steve Martin LP than Emi-nem. In the early days of Punderdome, the final two contend-ers faced off with whiteboards like any other round, but this routine changed a couple years in. One night, Jerzy and Rekha were up against each other in the last round and got exactly the same amount of applause. The crowd then started sponta-neously chanting "Pun-off! Pun-off!" as though they were all familiar with the O. Henry. Jo Firestone relented. She ordered Jerzy and Rekha to put their boards down and pun back and forth for two minutes or until one of them couldn't go any-more. The topic? Butts. After two minutes of verbal assplay, Jerzy won and a tradition was born.

This time, Jo chooses the Human Body, which means butts are again on the table. The two finalists square up, smiling. Isaac has been having a hell of a night and he's triumphed here before. But the Pundance Kid has had a strong showing and the crowd likes him. It could go either way.

Pundance strikes first, saying, "We'd better give these peo-ple a show, man, they paid an arm and a leg to be here."

Isaac nods. "If we go on too long, I don't think they'll be able to *stomach* any more."

"Should we even be out here yet," Pundance responds, "or should we still be *in-testin'*?"

As the two fire off and return each other's shots, I start to realize how unprepared I am for the O. Henry. In a breakneck exchange like this, you have to have several puns stashed at your disposal every moment, like a quiver of arrows. Not only that, but the judges at O. Henry will actually step in and point out that "an arm and a leg" is not a true pun since that expression refers to actual bodily appendages. I'm not ready for that. I hardly understand how anyone is.

The crowd is cheering when time runs out. Pundance turned in an incredible performance but I'd call this one for Isaac. Soon, a chant erupts: "Two more minutes! Two more minutes!"

Jo puts her hand over her face and shakes her head.

"You guys keep chanting and we're gonna be here all night."

Everybody screams even louder.

"All right," she yells, reaching for the timer. "Two more minutes, same topic. Go!"

"At the end of the day, you'll find I'm the bigger asshole," Pundance says immediately, and points at his eyeball. "*I-risk* a lot by saying that, but I believe it."

Isaac has a slightly trembling smile at the one-two punch, but he spits fire right back.

"As long as we're talking about eyes," he says, "you should shut up and be my *pupil.*"

The crowd explodes. Pundance waits for the laugh to die down, grinning like he has something ready for this.

"You guys went pretty crazy for that one, considering how *cornea* joke it was."

Something in the room ruptures and the air is now made of howling. Onstage, Isaac and Pundance have inched forward and are now in each other's faces.

"I think for me, trouble is *afoot,*" Isaac says, accurately.

When the timer goes off, Jo and Fred have to physically pull Isaac and Pundance apart. They're both smiling, and they clearly respect each other's skills, but the potency of the moment has them so keyed up it looks like a prelude to a fistfight. Instead, the pair breaks one of the only steadfast rules at Punderdome, and clasps each other in a bear hug.

The clap-o-meter goes center stage, and Isaac is up first. The Littlefield crowd is loud, but they're obviously holding back. Pundance is going to win.

He came here with no experience, like Punky Brewster, and somehow blew the roof off the place. While he may not have experience with pun competitions, I'm convinced he must have *some* experience onstage in one form or another. Pretty much everyone who kills here does. I'm just curious what his is.

After the show is over, Pundance, whose real name is Matt Chaves, is swallowed by a congratulatory swarm. A few minutes later, though, I jostle my way through and ask what he does.

He's a stand-up comedian. Of course he is.

# Semifinals

# 8

# @ THE JOKE OF MIDNIGHT

The crowd at Flappers Comedy Club in Burbank had no idea what they'd just gotten themselves into. Buying tickets to something called Uncle Clyde's Comedy Contest certainly counts as a *caveat emptor* situation, but nobody likely anticipated seeing the brawny bulk of Ben Ziek bound onstage to recite some puns.

Years before he discovered improv, Ziek made his live performance debut as a stand-up comedian. The foundation of his act back then was not puns, but rather impressions. He'd do Kermit the Frog singing "Rainbow Connection," and he had a mean Swedish Chef in his repertoire. He did stand-up in coffeehouses and college shows, once even opening for a popular campus headliner whose name he can't recall. By the time he cobbled together forty-five minutes, though, he was five years in, and most of his references were out of date. (Not Kermit, though. The relevance of Kermit the Frog will outlive us all.) Soon he gave up stand-up and started doing improv instead. But recently, he's been attempting a comeback.

With years of live performance under his belt, Ziek has started going to open mics at Flappers, along with the occasional booked gig. Instead of impressions, his new act capitalizes on his status as the World Champion of Pun Competitions. He started off writing a pun a day on Twitter in an effort to gather enough material to fill a few minutes. He only drew from his road-tested catalog of Punniest of Show routines for his set's grand finale. The crowd response so far has been substantially less batshit than what Ziek usually gets at O. Henry, but he plans on sticking with it. As Gary Hallock could vouch, though, stand-ups who try punning are usually way more successful than punsters who try stand-up.

Making a pun is comedy math, and all stand-up comedians are basically Isaac Newton. So when a stand-up comedian comes to a pun competition, she is more or less a wizard. Not only can stand-ups make quick, unexpected connections between words and ideas, they also have the instincts and timing to make anything sound like a punch line. In the same way punsters see word-contortion opportunities everywhere, a comic can funny up any sentence. The rhythm of a joke just becomes automatic, along with knowing which words to hit the hardest. And whether it's dealing with hecklers or doing crowd work, stand-up comedians always learn how to think on their feet and craft jokes out of whatever the moment provides them.

The Pundance Kid's victory at the first Dome of the year is an extreme example of how being a stand-up works in your favor at a pun competition. Sometimes the influence flows the other way, though. It certainly did in Darren Walsh's case.

Walsh was a pun-obsessed illustrator and animator living in the United Kingdom when he first set foot onstage to do stand-up in 2010. Rather than downplay his punning addiction, he made it the centerpiece of his act.

"A few of you are probably wondering why I have a projector here," he says in one routine, gesturing to a screen behind him as two words appear. "It's so I can literally *project 'I'll vomit.'*" He then waits a beat before adding, "That's a *sick* joke."

In his first few years of performing, Darren began earning awards and landing on Comics to Watch lists. When the UK Pun Championships launched in 2014, Darren won. The following year, he took his first solo show, *Punderbolt,* to Edinburgh Festival Fringe, the largest arts festival on the planet. It was a smash. At the time I got in touch with him, he was preparing to bring his second show, *S'Pun,* to the 2016 Fringe. Over just a handful of years, Darren had managed to build a thriving live act purely on the strength of puns.

"The UK comedy circuit is very different from the American one in that way," Darren says. "It might be because in America having 'a message' or an observation is more important, whereas here it's acceptable to just be silly."

Yes, clearly nobody in America would be interested in, say, three hundred pages of people being silly with puns. But Walsh might be onto something. Apart from the great ginger exception of Carrot Top, very few stateside stand-ups have puns in their acts. American comics seem acutely aware of puns' reputation as the lowest form of humor and so they strive to avoid being painted with that brush at all costs. The American comic most associated with wordplay in recent years, though, is probably Myq Kaplan. Whether he likes it or not.

Myq's initial claim to fame was placing fifth on *Last Comic Standing,* a TV show that emerged from the early 2000s gold rush to give every profession its own *American Idol*. Since then Myq has appeared on just about all the late-night talk shows and he's released several albums, a Comedy Central half hour, and a Netflix special. Although his style has definitely evolved along the way, each of these releases is at heart a playful celebration of language that includes some amount of punning.

"I want to assure you that of the number of puns that cross through my brain, only the smallest fraction come out of my mouth," Myq tells me as we swerve through traffic on the Brooklyn Queens Expressway.

If you've spent any time around Myq Kaplan onstage, online, or in a moving vehicle, the idea that the puns he shares are just the tip of some lexical iceberg is frankly terrifying.

We had planned to meet for coffee, but after e-mailing back and forth a few times, he invited me on his podcast instead. It was just easier that way. Going for coffee with a comedian and no microphone in 2016 is just an Unrecorded Podcast.

On Myq's show, *Hang Out with Me*, we talked about basically everything except puns. Now as he's driving me home from the studio in Astoria, the floodgates have opened. As he describes it, wordplay seems to be the background machinery constantly whirring in Myq's brain. Puns, spoonerisms, and portmanteaus are always sliding in and out of place like panels on a Japanese puzzle box. He's better equipped for it than most comics, too. In college, Myq discovered he loved diagramming sentences and learning the math of language, so he majored in linguistics. He wanted to know everything there is to know about the mechanism behind his particular form of mania.

"Certainly my interest in linguistics and my predilection for making the kind of jokes I make, those both spring from something inside," he says, the taillights from the car ahead reflecting off his glasses. "Those are both symptoms of the same internal disease."

Myq doesn't think he actually has a disease like *witzelsucht,* but rather an insistent compulsion. It's what drove him to title his first album *Vegan Mind Meld.* It's probably what also made him include on that album several religious frozen sperm puns in a row, including: *12 apopcicles, ejaculate conception, There's Something About the Virgin Mary,* and on and on. Myq is alternately in love with and wary of puns—especially considering how they're perceived in the United States. In order for that religious sperm bit to work during a set, he has to warn the crowd that they're about to go through a "pun jungle, or *pungle,*" and if they bear with him, it'll all be over soon.

These days, Myq has little use for puns in his act. Early in his career, if he thought of a solid original pun, he'd find space for it. As he amassed more material, though, he resisted being pigeonholed as a wordplay comic. His style became more geared toward "obsessive-compulsive parentheses disorder," where in the middle of one topic he'll burrow into a subtopic, and another subtopic within that one, like comedy *Inception.* His 2014 Netflix special is almost completely devoid of puns. After his closing joke mentions Hitler, though, he can't resist ending the special with, "I hope I didn't make you *Mein Kampf*-ortable."

Myq's punning is now mostly restricted to Twitter. Every other tweet comes emblazoned with the warning CUTE JOKE ALERT!, followed by something like "Elephants are good at multi-*tusking.*" Twitter is where comics like Myq go to bury the puns they can't use onstage and to lance the boil of wordplay building up beneath the surface. It's also where armchair comics proudly display their puns while playing along with *@Midnight,* a show where Myq has both worked as a warm-up comic and appeared as a guest. A lot of comedians dismiss the show's Twitter participation as amateur hour, a blizzard of timeline-clogging obnoxiousness. When those same comedians actually go on the show, though, they appear to enjoy themselves. Probably because it's the one place they can pun in public without warning people that it'll all be over soon.

BACK WHEN MYQ Kaplan was on *Last Comic Standing* and Darren Walsh was first trying out stand-up, Alex Blagg was nursing an obsession with Twitter games. They seemed to pop up out of nowhere once or twice a week and commandeer his entire feed. Something like #BreakfastFilms would appear and then a marquee comic like Patton Oswalt would tweet "*Omelet* the Right One In" and then, voilà, an amateur pun avalanche would come tumbling down. It was lightning in search of a bottle.

One day, Blagg wrote down in a Google doc of project ideas: "Game show where comedians compete at hashtag games." Then he forgot about it. Half a year later, when he was launching a production company, the screenwriter found himself combing through that Google doc for ideas to pitch. The Twitter game show looked like a winner. After troubleshooting through a few potential formats, Blagg and his partners eventually created a pilot episode. Wisely, they ditched the original name of the show: *Twitter Dome*.

The tone of the @*Midnight* pilot was arch and satirical. Its big conceptual joke was the idea of taking Twitter super, super seriously. The set looked like a James Bond villain's secret volcano-lair—as though contestants might be killed off if they couldn't come up with a decent #BreakfastFilm (e.g., *Waffle Metal Jacket*) fast enough. They've since dialed back on the smoke machines and lasers, surgically removing the ironic quote marks from the competition. By the time *@Midnight* made it to air, the series resembled more of a gamified *Daily Show* with a heavy Internet focus. Of course, the viewers playing Hashtag Wars at home still ended up taking the competition as seriously as the pilot suggested they should. Some contestants did, too.

"I really wasn't trying to lose, " Jen Kirkman says in the hall backstage. She has just lost on *@Midnight,* playing against Paul F. Tompkins and Randy Sklar.

"Oh, I know you weren't!" Paul says, a smile breaking out beneath his riverboat gambler's mustache. "I kept looking over at you and you were like fucking *into* it."

The two walk so loosely beside each other, it's obvious there's no tension between them. Neither cares about winning a game as much as they care about helping each other put on a funny show. But Paul is right. There was a moment during the taping when I saw a predatory look flash across Jen's face—a look I associated with Punderdome. It was the kind of severe smile someone about to crack a joke makes after sliding from *They're gonna love this* to *They'd* better *love this.* That's the unexpected side effect that happens when comedy meets competition.

Continuing down the hall, we pass a section on the backside of the set where all the contestants so far have graffitied their names in marker. It's sprawling enough to look like a mass memorial for the Comedian Wars of the 2010s. At this moment, *@Midnight* is nearing its four-hundredth episode. That's four hundred hashtags. Four hundred For the Win rounds. An incalculable sum of ad-libs from whip-smart host Chris Hardwick, the comedian and podcaster who is so integral to the

show, his name is in the official title, *@Midnight with Chris
Hardwick.* Since its debut in 2013 *@Midnight* has brought consistently high ratings, earned an Emmy, and more important
for our purposes, it's turned the Internet into a pun competition just about every night of the week.

*@Midnight* is an impressive showcase of just how funny
stand-up comics can be without any prepared material.
They make one joke after another, round after round, and
they make it look easy. Unlike the devoted hordes contrib-
uting #SadTVShows and #RuinAChildrensBook entries from
home, the comics actually have a ticking clock and a live audience. (I arrived at *NooseRadio* and *Red Vag of Courage,* respectively, only after several minutes of deep thought.) It's the
difference between singing in the shower and, well, singing
in the shower on a comedy game show on TV. When I visit
the set during the week of *@Midnight's* first-ever Tournament
of Champions, I hope to find out how the show's best get so
damn good at it.

AFTER ARRIVING AT the enormous, cotton-candy-colored Stage
2 of Hollywood Center Studios—where *I Love Lucy* was filmed,
I'm told twice—the first thing I want to see is the writers' room.
It's an option that apparently is not on the table, though.

"We sacrifice goats in there," Alex Blagg says. Further prod-
ding reveals that the room is sealed with bureaucratic red tape
from the network. Alex's hands are tied. Instead, he shows me
the crafts service table—which has a Dionysian smorgasbord of
Slim Jims, Fritos, and peanut M&M's, along with a sloppy joe
maker—and tells me about the writers' room.

In the same way a punch line is only as strong as its setup, the comics on @*Midnight* only get to tomahawk-dunk most of their jokes with an alley-oop from the writers. Plenty of jokes naturally arise from the guests' interplay with the host and each other, but the jokes they make in the rapid-fire games have been reverse engineered with precision.

The writing staff, whose room I am not allowed within, is split just about evenly between stand-up and improv performers. Some of the more established ones, like Shelby Fero and Blaine Capatch, occasionally compete on the show, but all the writers have a chance to play the game every single day. It's their job to field-test each segment and make sure that night's guests will be able to extract enough jokes out of it. A Hashtag War, for instance, generally won't make it on the air unless ten to fifteen minutes of spitballing in the room yields forty to fifty decent jokes from the writers. This is exactly what the O. Henry committee does with new pun categories before approving them, although something tells me this is probably the funnier place to be.

Compared to how vast the audience appears in panning shots on a flatscreen, the seating area for @*Midnight* now looks about the size of a modest sandbox. (It's amazing what can be accomplished with soaring camera jibs.) The set itself looks bigger, though. It's encased by glass walls streaked with white pulsating lines and circles meant to suggest circuitry, but which look more like a tube map of London. A handler escorts me to a seat a few rows back from the front, where the people with the most visually interesting hair are concentrated.

"You will be on TV more than everybody else," a refrigerator-size warm-up comic named Roger tells them. "So no resting bitch face." Everyone laughs, implicitly agreeing to the terms.

Chris Hardwick, or Papa Bear as Roger calls him, is instantly amped as he settles in at his podium, a steel sandwich with two Facebook-blue lights as the bread. With a background in improv, stand-up, and futilely attempting to distract horny viewers from cohost Jenny McCarthy on MTV's *Singled Out*, he is an ideal host—for this show, and, hypothetically, for Punderdome. He's quick, he's generous with whoever else is onstage, and he's nowhere near too cool to make puns.

In his nightly uniform of well-fitted suit, skinny tie, and carefully disheveled hair, Chris is normally the most dapper on the show. Tonight, however, Paul F. Tompkins is wearing a straight-up black tuxedo with a violet pocket square, decisively winning any unofficial sartorial competition. Jen Kirkman and Randy Sklar look perfectly fine, but the disparity between them and Paul makes it seem like either they or he were deceived about a dress code in an elaborate prank.

When Chris announces the Hashtag War, I'm sad to see that it's not even slightly punnable. Instead, tonight's entry, #IfTrumpWins, makes good on the universal truth that Donald Trump is the most reliable joke target of 2016. The very next game, however, produces almost exclusively pun responses.

The game is called Cobragator, a tribute to the Roger Corman movies on Syfy that pair two unlikely killer creatures with the most indifferently produced special effects money can buy. The comics have to come up with as many hybrid monsters of their own as they can in sixty seconds.

"*AntelOprah*," Randy offers.

"*Dracullama*," Paul says, with a silent film eyebrow-raise.

"Scott *Baio-wolf*," Jen calls out, looking embarrassed. Paul cracks up, but it's difficult to tell whether it's because of what she said or how she said it.

Jen is soon dismissed from the show, ahead of the game-ending For the Win challenge, which is always between the two finalists. There's a moment afterward, when she's still standing at her podium, bathed in awkward red dismissal light, crossing her arms and closing her eyes in a mummy pose. Paul then wins the challenge, which is decided, Punderdome style, by audience applause.

The taping goes so smoothly, you can see why it's almost the 400th episode. Now that it's over, though, I go backstage to see if I can get these comedians to talk about puns.

The green room at the studio is actually powder blue, with a wet bar that has thin neon piping throughout. There's water, wine, soda, and Red Bull in compact refrigerators, along with all kinds of breads and cheeses in birdcage-size cheese domes. A PR rep for the show narrates his decision to eat carbs and then chastises himself for it. Paul has loosened his tie now, and up close, I can see he's wearing a lapel button adorned with the logo of his podcast, *Spontaneanation*. (All three have podcasts, naturally. It's never a question of "Does this comedian have a podcast?" but "How many?")

Once everybody arranges themselves across the couches, I ask how being a stand-up helps with thinking of funny things in the moment.

"The longer you've had experience being onstage, the more you can do ten things at once with your mind," Jen says. "Not make a stupid face on camera, think of your next joke, come up with a tag for the joke, and quickly recover if it doesn't go well."

I can do maybe two things onstage at a time; one of them is "not fall off it," and even that's no sure bet.

"It also helps if you're able to write onstage," Paul says. "In my earliest days, I think I was able to project a confidence that

I did not necessarily have, so that bought me time to think, but as I've gotten genuinely more comfortable onstage over the years, I'm better in the moment at coming up with things."

"That's how I write all the time," Jen says. "I'll have a rough skeleton of what I want to say and then the pressure of being out there motivates me and makes me feel confident to say stuff. I'm less confident writing something and then going on-stage with that attitude of 'I think this is funny!' I'd rather just go for it and let it come out naturally."

The pressure of being "out there" has apparently had a different effect on me so far than it has had on Jen Kirkman. Mainly it's made me second-guess every potential pun as really dumb and scurry away from the microphone like it's on fire. At the same time, though, I've seen people like Jerzy and Isaac perform some okay-at-best puns with a sterling conviction that earns them the room on a platter.

"Does a joke ever pop in your head on *@Midnight,* and you don't really think it's good but it's your turn so you just deliver the shit out of it?" I ask.

"There might be a thing that you don't really have time to think twice about," Paul says, reclining in his seat. "And you've just gotta be, like, 'I'm gonna sell this like it's the funniest thing I've ever said.'"

"Or you don't sell it," Randy says. "You sell it as horrible and then *that* gets a laugh."

"Sometimes selling a really bad joke you just made up, if it's bad enough and you let on you know that it's bad, is better than landing a well-written joke," Jen says.

One of the most striking things about Punderdome is how earnest it is. Nearly everyone goes there because they unabashedly enjoy puns. Punning ironically there is like crying in a monsoon. In other situations, people use puns as arch antijokes to make someone laugh at how unfunny what they're saying is. Comedy writers, especially. Seasoned comedians hear so many jokes, sometimes the only way to make them laugh is with how intensely unfunny something is—say, a pun. But those same puns would be received sincerely at Punderdome or the O. Henry, getting laughs for a different reason. Which brings me to the fourth kind of Bad Pun: the Look Ma No Hands. This one comes down to intention, and the way you sell it.

When Mitt Romney was vying for the presidency in 2011, he suggested during a campaign stop at a diner that the cook should serve eggs Benedict on hubcaps because—and this is indeed a quote—"There's no *plates* like *chrome* for the *hollandaise*." Nearly fifty-seven million people still voted for him, but I like to think the joke had some kind of impact at the polls. Whoever gave Romney that pun to use had awkwardly stuffed three breakfast puns into a verbal turducken, which he deployed in hopes of coming across as folksy. It did not work.

On the other end of the spectrum, the late, brilliant comedy writer Harris Wittels once put three breakfast puns together hilariously. During a visit to the podcast *Comedy Bang Bang*, Wittels said with zero affect, "I wanna open a Jamaican/Irish/Spanish small plate breakfast restaurant and call it *Tapas* the Morning to *Jah*." Immediately afterward, another guest on the show, the musician Annie Clark, let out a groan as if she'd been gut-punched. It's a complimentary groan, somehow. Wittels's pun is just as much of a stretch as Romney's, but in some indefinable way, it's clear he knows that.

The lack of agenda is why his joke is bracing anticomedy while Romney's is just a bad pun that appears to be the source of much unearned pride.

"So you can sell a bad joke, but what about a pun?" I ask the group. "Do you ever make puns in general?"

"If I did puns in my stand-up, I think it would just come off kinda corny and dishonest and 'who cares,' but it's a fun thing to do," Jen says. "It's not necessarily always appropriate for the public, but on *@Midnight* it works well because you're doing it so fast."

Paul and Randy both nod vigorously.

"I'm not a huge fan of puns just for the sake of puns," Paul says. "To me, a pun is: These two things sound alike, that's the end of the humor. What I do like is wordplay, and I think that although there are a lot of puns on this show, there are also a lot of turns of phrase and it's the way words are put together and to me that's something else."

With perhaps a touch of Romney-like pride, I explain how varied the turns of phrase are at Punderdome—that all these spontaneous puns are either couched in classic joke structure or linked together in a story. Nobody can even pretend this sounds like a place they'd like to visit. The room stays silent for a moment before Jen speaks up.

"Everybody makes fun of *Sex and the City* for having a lot of puns," she says, "and I think of this one scene everybody talks about in the second movie, when Samantha goes 'Lawrence of *My Labia*.'"

Everybody nods with recognition. This line got singled out and excoriated by critics when the film was released. When I eventually speak to Greg Behrendt, a stand-up comedian who consulted on *Sex and the City* and coined the phrase "He's just not that into you," he confirms that the puns were his absolute least favorite part of the show by far.

"That line had to go through so many drafts of a script, rehearsals, it had so many moments to be killed," Jen continues, "but people decided: 'This is funny, and not ironically.'"

Paul and Randy both laugh a little.

"If I said Lawrence of My Labia on @*Midnight*, though, it would be funny," Jen says. "Because you'd be, like, 'She thought of that in two seconds and she knows she's being silly.' It wasn't like a writer who gets paid a lot of money wrote that for a character and was, like, 'Let's make sure Lawrence of My Labia gets all the way to filming.'"

"And if you do any pun as Johnny Carson, I think that works, too," Randy says. When he tries out Lawrence of My Labia with a dead-on Johnny Carson, everybody laughs.

"I would've loved that movie so much if Samantha busted out a Carson," Paul says.

"After all these years," Jen adds, "Samantha's finally comfortable in her own skin as a woman. 'Girls, now that I'm fifty-five and I've hit menopause, I wanna show you another side of myself.

'I do impressions of men.'"

"Who'd be the Ed McMahon of *Sex and the City*?" Jen asks.

Everybody says "Charlotte" at the exact same moment, which ironically seems like the button on a scene in an episode of *Sex and the City*. Then they all continue to do what comics do and riff *Sex and the City* jokes for a couple more minutes.

REGISTRY FOR THE O. Henry Pun-Off will be open soon, with the competition itself just over a month away. Punsters across the nation are preparing themselves to do battle in Austin, and the digital duel of *@Midnight* is a decent way to start practicing.

As incentive to play along, the show's social media producer singles out an exceptional tweet each night and flashes it across the screen during the episode. The gravitational pull of *@Midnight* bragging rights is strong enough to lure almost every self-respecting punster into its orbit, beyond just those who are training to compete. Neither the practice-averse Punky Brewster nor the overachieving Ben Ziek can resist the show's siren song. Ask any Domer or O. Henry affiliate under thirty-five and they've likely tried to get their tweet featured on *@Midnight*.

Taking the time to craft #SuckyActionMovie puns can't really prepare anyone for the speed volleying at O. Henry or in the final round of Punderdome, though. The best way to do that is with a flesh-and-blood human person, preferably one who doesn't hate puns. Tim used to practice on the roof of his apartment with his friend Black Punther. They would smoke a joint, come up with topics, and go back and forth, flexing the lexicon. The goal was to keep up the rhythm of a natural conversation, so that crafting a punny response felt as natural as talking. This technique might not have unearthed the greatest puns ever—they are lost to the ages now—but because of the impairment, the two felt like hilarious geniuses, and both did well at subsequent Punderdomes. When hanging out was inconvenient, the two would text puns back and forth—and since hanging out is always inconvenient now that Black Punther has moved to Cincinnati, they still do have textual pun-offs sometimes.

Ally practices this way, too, minus the marijuana. Usually, though, it's by accident. Conversations with friends will just lapse into punspeak until a topic is completely drained of puns. Sometimes it happens in person and sometimes over text. When two pun champions are friends, like Ally is with Nikolai, any digital exchange on any topic can go straight off the rails and turn into this:

[tbh I like this weather]

[Perfect for tea drinking, of course you do]

[And for going to the post office to pick up a rain jacket. O the irony]

[I-rainy]

[Spoken like a raining pun champion]

[Defending my title pourly]

[I'm losing my cloudt]

[Precipitating a loss at the next dome]

[Maybe I'll wind]

[Snow way]

[Guess it depends weather I'm there or not]

[These things are hard to forecast]

[It's knot that hard]

[We should hang out mon-soon]

[Soon, ah. Me, you mean?]

[Yes, her-I-can see soon?]

[You're really flooding my text inbox]

And on and on until the phone itself revolts by freezing up.

Gary Hallock is striving to find ways to build a similar practice element into the Facebook page for Punsters United Nearly
Yearly (PUNY). The main way he does so is with pun prompts.
Twice a week, Hallock posts a tried-and-true category, allowing
group members to compete for "likes." Open up the page any
day and you might see the image of a fuel gauge, with the cap-
tion, "Here's a topic we can *oil* pun on!" The jokes soon spew
out in a geyser of vaudevillian word soup. "This topic should
be a *gas!*" one person writes, possibly from inside the Bazooka
Joe wrapper factory in 1956. "The odometer on my old car is so
accurate . . . truly an *honest engine!*" another adds, instead of
not doing that. Training this way can be helpful if for no other
reason than as an endurance exercise—a flu shot inoculation
against the pun virus you might contract at O. Henry.

To prepare people for real-time punning, though, Gary went
a step further and developed a way to duplicate the experience
of live competition. In the lead-up to the last couple O. Henrys, Hallock organized what he calls Punslingers Stimulators,
where two punsters can meet up in a Facebook chat window at
a specified time and duke it out. Although this method is more

accurate than punning against a stopwatch or tweeting jokes into the void for *@Midnight,* there's really nothing that can re-create the pressure of standing in front of a crowd of hundreds, at the mercy of the masses. Being in a pun competition is truly the best possible preparation for a pun competition.

# 9

## THE CAULIFLOWER'S CUMIN
## FROM INSIDE THE HOUSE

It didn't occur to me there was any chance I wouldn't make it into the O. Henry—right until the moment I didn't make it.

This year, for the first time ever, the event's organizing body opted to use a lottery system for admission. Demand for the World Series of pun competitions had simply become too rabid for the first-come-first-served days of yore. A flotilla of qualified but slow-fingered punsters were being left in the lurch, and something had to change. Converting to a lottery system would ostensibly level the playing field. Everyone who wanted in would have the same forty-eight-hour window to apply online, with competitors selected at random. Speed had been removed as a factor, leaving O. Henry admission in the hands of Tyche, Greek goddess of chance and providence.

At 11:59 A.M. on April first, my click-finger hovered diligently over my laptop, triggering a muscle memory of fruitless attempts to score Radiohead tickets. A minute passed and registration was under way. I swiftly navigated all appropriate fields, submitting myself for Punniest of Show and Punslingers. There is no way I could have gone any faster, barring fingertip steroids. Three days later, though, I still received twin e-mail responses letting me know I'd been wait-listed for both events. It was like getting anorexic envelopes from Harvard and Yale at once, only far nerdier. While almost everyone I'd ever met before this past year might send a cease and desist letter upon being asked to enter the Pun Olympics, I was livid at the injustice of being denied.

As the other Punderdomers received similar e-mails, updates began pouring in on an O. Henry Gmail thread like real-time election results.

Tim and Sam, who worked together at Brokelyn, learned of their fate at the same time. Tim got into both events; Sam got into neither.

"The patriarchy strikes again!" Tim crowed.

Moments later, Nikolai revealed that he'd been double wait-listed like I had.

"The patriarchy has failed me," he said.

Ally didn't make it into either event. Neither did Ariel or Jordan. Isaac got Punslingers, but not Punniest of Show. Jerzy would be competing in both. I didn't need to reach out to Ben Ziek to find out whether he'd made it in.

Obviously, this was horseshit. The heavy hitters were getting a pass no matter what, and the rest of us were being shat out through some unknowable sorting hat. I couldn't really blame the committee for this. Of course the O. Henry faithful would prefer to see Ziek or Jerzy face off against other known quantities, rather than go up against click-happy randos. But why did they have to start filtering now—the year so many Domers were planning to compete? Didn't they realize the social sacrifices I'd personally made to get ready for O. Henry? That very weekend, while waiting to hear back, I'd been at a restaurant in the East Village, sharing a molcajete of guacamole and declared of its tame heat: "This is like Fisher Price: My First Spicy. It's Fisher Spice." I said that out loud, to *people,* and I had no idea if I was being ironic like Jen Kirkman or if I was being sincere. I just knew it was difficult to beat back this reflex after saying these kinds of things at Punderdome had made the crowd laugh.

It was unclear how many people on the wait list would find their way into the thirty-two available slots for either event, but considering that so many of us just in Brooklyn were jockeying to get in, my odds didn't look great. If I were to put together a Punniest of Show routine now, it would be for a competition I might not end up in. And this unfortunate possibility was hanging over my head the very next night at Punderdome.


SAM IS THE first person I bump into at Littlefield that night, loose tufts of blond hair spilling out of her black knit cap, nervously devouring a Garfield-colored cardboard prism she claims is vegan pizza. Sam's nervous because this is her first time competing in months, since her schedule became increasingly hectic. She'd recently started moving beyond Subreddit Live, the occasional revue she hosted with Ally, to experiment with other shows around the city. It had gone encouragingly well so far. Before drifting briefly away from Punderdome, though, Sam had become a six-time champion, making her nerves tonight kind of redundant. Or at least as redundant as vegan pizza.

Sam has a story about the first pun she ever made. She was

scarfing down a fish dinner one night, at ten years old, and she noticed a piece of salmon wedged into the shape of a cigar. On impulse, she picked it up and held it to her lips, Groucho style, and something just clicked. Her wordplay instinct booted up right then, and she announced to the table, "Hey: smoked salmon!" Her parents—both major fans of puns, salmon, and Sam—were delighted and proud, and an obsession was born.

In high school, Sam studied etymology. She began to see the connections between words—the way *police* related to *policy*, and both derived from the Greek word *polis*, meaning "city." Sam became a Latin nerd and a member of the Classics Club. She also began writing plays for the annual Classics competition, which was how she first found her calling. Although she's an editor at Brokelyn and a Jill of all trades in New York comedy shows, Sam considers herself first and foremost a playwright. The world of theater is, to her, an endless laboratory in which to experiment with language. Sam loves stretching out words to investigate what's inside them—and a lot of times, it turns out being puns. Her plays tend to have more puns than the average theater piece—not as linguistic accents, but essential ingredients. One of her plays, about a woman who is the messiah of postmodernism, is entirely composed of puns. It may sound like a far cry from typical theater, but it's surprisingly not as far as one might think.

Theatrical history is littered with wordplay, much of it from Shakespeare himself. Picture the most acclaimed playwright of all time in his bedroom, dreaming up puns while dripping quill ink on his puffy tunic sleeves. That totally happened. A lot! When Thersites of *Troilus and Cressida* says, "But yet you look not well upon him; for, whomsoever you take him to be, he is Ajax," it's not just because a character is named "Ajax," but because "a jakes" meant a public toilet back then. Never mistake the Bard for someone above poop and fart jokes. He couldn't resist them. Perhaps it was a trait he picked up from reading Chaucer, who made flatulent puns on "a penny farthing" with alarming frequency. But whether the puns were dirty or not, Shakespeare clearly loved his verbal Russian nesting dolls, and it's a tradition that continues to this day with many playwrights besides Sam Corbin. It's also something that's found its way into that most modern version of the Globe Theatre: your TV. Or more likely, your laptop.

TV shows aren't necessarily the current analog to plays in Shakespeare's day—that would be the cinema of Nicolas Cage—but the narrative ones do share the same basic purpose, despite being shorter and absent of iambic pentameter. Some also share a dedication to punning, whether the writers admit it or not. But since a play is written only once, and *Sex and the City* generously spans seven seasons and two films, the writers on punny TV shows have to be able to crank out wordplay all day. The staff on certain sitcoms, and pretty much every late-night talk show, understands the pressure of a pun competition as much as anyone who's ever graced the O. Henry stage, if not more so. Instead of competing for bragging rights, these people are trying to satisfy critics and fans and also keep their jobs.

*Bob's Burgers* is a whimsical animated sitcom about a quirky family who own a burger joint in a quaint seaside town. Pitched at grown-up goofballs, the show is also kid-friendly, buoyed by schmaltz-free positivity and catchy original tunes. Also, its voice cast is basically a Bonnaroo tent of hip comics. *Bob's Burgers* premiered on Fox in 2011 and had all the makings of one of those brilliant-but-canceled one-season wonders, lamented in comment threads for years to come. But somehow, network

TV got this one right. *Bob's Burgers* defied the odds, surviving seven seasons and counting. One of the defining characteristics that's helped the show thrive, though, is its systemic punniness.

That isn't hyperbole, either. *Bob's Burgers* goes far beyond a mere fondness for wordplay; it's more like a devotion, in the religious sense, with one of those calendars that has sunflowers and mountain vistas for every month. Puns don't just pop up in the dialogue occasionally—although they sure do—they're also embedded into the very fabric of the series. Each episode has a literal pun quota, with standing reservations at three separate points in the script. When the show's writers have to produce these puns on a deadline, they become contestants in, well, if not exactly a pun competition, at least a pun challenge. I decided to find out how much that process changed between a Burbank office and a Brooklyn stage.

BENTO BOX ENTERTAINMENT is headquartered on a tree-lined street in the least glamorous section of Burbank. It looks from a distance more like an elementary school than the home of an animated comedy powerhouse. On the inside, though, there's no mistaking it for anyplace else. Life-size cardboard standees of Bob and Linda Belcher greet you at the door, the characters coated in muddy twigs and leaves as per the episode "A River Runs Through Bob." Hanging above a chocolate leather couch are framed cover stories from *Variety* and *Entertainment Weekly,* and assorted industry backslaps for a 2014 Emmy win. The entire Belcher family's faces are also splashed across the elliptic curve of the reception desk. (Linda's is obscured by a Slimer-green handwritten sign directing staffers to where they can purchase Girl Scout cookies.) The studio produces other shows, but *Bob's Burgers* is the clear breadwinner.

While I'm waiting to meet Wendy Molyneux, one-half of the show's celebrated sister act writing duo, I sneak a peek around the corner. What's on the wall in the next room makes me gasp audibly: a real-life Burger of the Day board.

On each episode, Chef Bob will at some point scrawl a new culinary concoction on the wall of his restaurant, one of the show's regularly scheduled pun moments. The freshly chalked menu might promote The Last of the Mo-jicama Burger (comes with jicama), the Beets of Burden Burger (comes with too many beets), or perhaps most impressively, the Cauliflower's Cumin from Inside the House Burger (comes with cauliflower and cumin). This part of the show is so beloved and Internet famous that the writers published *The Bob's Burgers Burger Book: Real Recipes for Joke Burgers* around the time of my visit.

The Burger of the Day concept was in place right from the pilot episode, where it served as a plot point. Bob has a good chuckle over his latest creation, the New Baconings burger (comes with bacon), but his pathologically mischievous daughter, Louise, erases and replaces it with the Child Molester (comes with candy). On the day the restaurant is being inspected, no less. You can probably guess whether or not hijinks ensue. In the following episode, Louise again switches the Burger of the Day, this time from Never Been Feta, to Foot Feta-ish, but the gimmick of Louise interfering with the sign stopped at this point. The sign itself remained a staple of the show, though, preparing viewers for all the puns to come, burger based and otherwise.

At the Bento studio, on a mustard-yellow wall, there's a section of chalk paint with a ketchup-red border that allows anyone to leave behind a Burger of the Day idea. The one on display now is a tribute to last week's Leap Day, the Leap Pan-year Burger (comes with paneer and *extra d'ai*oli). I'm just starting to think of possible replacements, when I hear my name called out.

Wendy Molyneux has oatmeal blond hair, a warm smile, and simultaneously projects the demeanor of a rascally neighbor kid and her mom. She seems like someone you might steal an expensive bottle of champagne with when the wedding bartender isn't looking.

"Those burger puns are hard for me," she says, gesturing toward the board. "There's only so many ingredients, and you can only use kale so many times before people start to notice."

I'd sort of assumed all the writers were natural pun virtuosos, so this is a surprise.

Wendy asks if I want the tour. Of course I want the tour. As we walk down the hallway by the writers' offices, I see a corkboard full of press clippings. Whoever at *Boston Herald* interviewed Eugene Mirman—the comedian who voices Bob's lovable dunce son, Gene—couldn't resist the pun headline, MIRMAN ESPECIALLY SAUCY ON 'BURGERS.' To the left of this clip, though, is the honeypot: a sign-up sheet for Burger of the Day pitches. It's a single page abutted with runoff suggestions on pink and yellow Post-its. A few pitches are crossed out with the word *used* next to them. Others are too ridiculous to make on air, including the Flux Ca-cheeseburger (comes with McFlys), three in a row based on the band Pearl Jam, and my personal favorite, I Know, Ryyye-t? (served on rye). All these suggestions are either alternates or inside jokes. The writers are expected to submit their top-choice puns with each script.

*Bob's Burgers* works like most other sitcoms in that the writer assigned to an episode goes off alone to write a draft, then everyone else injects it with notes and jokes. After that, it's revise and repeat, until the script is optimal. The assigned writer on each *Bob's,* though, must also produce three or four options for each recurring pun, and then the show's creator, Loren Bouchard, picks his favorites. Aside from the Burger of the Day, the other regular puns are Storefronts and Rat Vans, both of which arrive during the opening credits.

Because Bob's Burgers is apparently under a witch's curse, the credits depict the restaurant alternately overrun by rats, lit on fire, and finally crushed by a utility pole. As these disturbances occur, a new set of surrounding businesses springs up on either side. The one on the left is always a funeral home called It's Your Funeral, but the one on the right has a new name each week—a used appliance store called A Fridge Too Far, maybe, or a boxing gym called I'd Hit That. When the rats infest, an extermination van immediately pulls up in front of the building, always adorned with a name like Wild Wild Pest, or Last of the Mousehicans. The writers need to keep replenishing puns for these services, week after week.

"Usually what's helpful is that there's a lot of us," Wendy says. "If you can't really think of puns, you get a room—"

"Get a room!" a smirking dude declares while walking by.

"—and I'm not good at them so usually there's like four or five of us sitting around, pitching puns."

"That sounds like a pun competition almost," I point out.

"Well, yes, but we're not trying to top each other. It just helps generate ideas, being around other people," she continues. "If someone does a yarn store pun, you might come up with one, too. If someone does a better one than you, it's like 'Oh good, there's a better one!'"

Wendy and the other staffers' ability to wield wordplay is what led Loren Bouchard to build puns into every episode. When I talk to him a few days later, he confirms that although the Burger of the Day pun was always going to be a weekly feature, the storefront and rat van puns developed because he was so impressed with his team. The storefronts were originally just places nobody would want to live or work near, like Bass Drum Emporium or a raccoon sanctuary. Over the first season, though, Loren started leaning toward punnier names, and the writers began pitching more of them, like Maxi Pads Large Apartment Rentals. Gradually, puns were codified as the letter of the law. It took longer for Loren to realize he was also leaving money on the table, pun-wise, with the rat vans. At first, the vans always just read Rats All Folks. By season two, Loren was confident they could be new each week.

"It's the pleasure of being around these people who are good with puns, which makes you want to see what they can do," he says. "It's really impressive to me when it comes out so fast and you say 'Jesus, how did you make that connection?'"

I tell Loren he should come to Punderdome if he's ever in New York.

Eventually, Wendy's sister, Lizzie, joins us. She's slightly younger, has blond hair, too, but more a Disney Princess, hay-colored blond than Wendy's, and the two share a similar fun energy. Lizzie asks if I've seen the writers' room yet and I haven't, so we head toward it. We walk past a bank of cubicles where computer animators are sketching characters from the show. It feels inappropriate, somehow, like seeing muppets hung on coatracks during production breaks at *Sesame Street*. Eventually we get to a room painted the same tapioca color as the inside of Bob's Burgers. Beyond a set of perpendicular couches, the back wall is an illustrated facsimile of the restaurant's countertop: napkin dispensers, condiment sets, and all. When they're up against a deadline, this is where the writers get together to brainstorm puns.

"If it's a Burger of the Day or rat van, at least you have a starting point," Lizzie says, plopping down on the couch. Right above her shoulder is a whiteboard where every episode title is scribbled in colored markers. Almost all of them are puns.

"You can either go with burger ingredients or types of vermin. You come up with 'mouse,' which rhymes with 'house,' so you think of which movies have 'house' in the title," Lizzie says. "For a storefront, I feel like there's two schools of thought: you can just go off the name of a store that already exists—like Bloodbath and Beyond—or you can come up with a product another store could sell. Like, one writer had the idea Bronanas: Bananas for Men, but it didn't go through, because Loren doesn't do other foods for storefronts."

This is one of a few steadfast logic rules dictating how these gags work. Another is that the names of storefronts have to be semiplausible. Loren would never approve A Bird in the Band: Guitars for Birds, for instance, because nobody sells guitars to birds. (Yet.) Another rule is that the Burger of the Day has to sound at least somewhat delicious, because in the world of the show, Bob is low-key, the Mario Batali of burgers. The writers have to keep these constraints in mind when coming up with puns, all while trying to avoid pitching a repeat.

"You could also just start with a phrase, like 'Go big or go home,' and go from there," Wendy says, making me suddenly sure there's an episode titled Go Bob or Go Home. "What was that one you did recently, Lizzie?"

"Ton in the Oven: A Store for Large Babies," she says cheerfully. "I hate to admit it but I have googled, like, 'popular phrases in the '90s' to come up with ideas."

She also uses rhyming dictionaries, IMDb, and idiomatic encyclopedias, just like the copyeditors at the *New York Post* when they're making headlines. Once the writers have enough potential ideas, the selection process for puns is as hierarchical as it is at the *Post*, too, with Loren Bouchard getting the final say. If all the effort that goes into making each *Bob's Burgers* pun shows, though, sometimes it's all the better.

"We do try to get the sweatiest pun possible," Wendy Molyneux says. "We're not trying to get a laugh with the pun—we're trying to get a laugh with the sweatiness of the pun."

Some puns are like IKEA furniture where there aren't enough cam locks or nut sleeves and the instructions are missing a page and also you're drunk, but you still attempt assembly. When you can just feel every expended neuron and synapse that went into a clusterfuck pun like Mitt Romney's "There's no plates like chrome for the hollandaise," the joke becomes the effort itself. The only way to save an overwrought pun is by disowning it with your delivery. That's why it's easier to have a character on a show make a sweaty pun than to make one yourself. Some element of the character can make it funny that she is putting together this janky verbal bedframe, whereas when it's, say, me in real life, describing the moment the bar runs out of limes as "lime-eleven," you can't really hide behind a character.

If your name is attached to an episode of a show you wrote, however, you can't really hide, either. At least that's why Sean Gray, a coproducer on HBO's *Veep,* is taken aback when I tell him he's the author of one of that show's punniest episodes. He is taken further aback when I send over a lengthy list of puns from it.

"That's probably too many puns," he says over the phone from London. "It's a lot."

Like *Bob's Burgers* before it, *Veep* also had a pun as a plot point in its first episode. The vice president, played with acerbic intensity by Julia Louis-Dreyfus, gets into hot water, public opinion–wise, after using the expression "hoisted by our own *retard*" in a speech. It was a proper starter pistol shot for a show that thrives on vulgar pun insults.

The reason *Veep* is so heavy on puns is because the creator and showrunner for the first four seasons, Armando Iannucci, demanded every line on the show be as sharp as possible. It was not an uncommon request, but his approach was unique. Iannucci instituted a policy of what some might call excessive redrafting. The show's writers constantly retool scripts as they go along to make sure the dialogue is always crackling. As they run through draft after draft, they accumulate as many as a couple dozen alt versions of each scene. The puns then ultimately found their way in after Armando gave the frequent script note "more color." That's why characters often say things like "shituation room" the moment a scene even approaches having a dull moment. The puns are flourishes, rarely punch lines.

The main challenge with putting puns into a narrative show, though, is making sure they stay in keeping with the characters.

"All the characters speak in very specific ways so you want

to make sure the gags and wordplay are organic to them," Sean Gray says. "Fortunately with *Veep*, the world of politics is obsessed with jargon so it doesn't feel out of place."

The character on *Veep* who tends to pull the most punny insults into his orbit is White House aide, and grade-A jackass, Jonah Ryan. When I ask Sean about how collaborating helps create puns for the show, he singles out something called the Jonad Files. This is a fictitious document for which several characters have contributed Jonah nicknames, making fun of his gangly appearance and general weasel factor. The Jonad Files are only revealed during a court scene toward the end of the fourth season, which turns into a pun run of very dirty names like Jizzy Gillespie and Spewbacca. Sean and all the other *Veep* writers worked on this list together and had a blast doing it. The kicker to the scene, though, which Sean wrote himself, is most revealing about how puns can reflect character. Eventually, Jonah offers an example of the kind of nickname he prefers, "Tall McCarthy." There is nothing funny about that pun on its own, but in the context of this particular person trying to get a flattering nickname admitted on court record, it's hilarious.

The puns on *Bob's Burgers* are reflective of its characters, too. Not the storefronts and rat vans, perhaps, but the Burger of the Day is certainly a showcase for Bob's sense of humor, and his love of puns informs the rest of the family.

"I think Bob does not enjoy puns ironically," Wendy says near the end of our tour. "I think he enjoys puns sincerely while the rest of the family thinks they're groanworthy. So even the kids do pun jokes, but usually with a little nod toward the fact that they're sweaty, whereas Bob doesn't have that nod."

Of course he doesn't. Bob is a drunken IKEA craftsman with his puns, jamming words together whether they fit or not.

His sincerity is adorable—the exact opposite of Mitt Romney's faux-folksiness. It would also probably slay at Punderdome.

DURING FRED'S WARM-UP at Littlefield in April, I'm waiting near the front of the stage with Sam and Nikolai. Sam is still experiencing a butterfly stomach-swarm.

"I should be all right, as long as the category isn't, like, baseball," she says. "But I don't know. I really don't know."

The crowd is as massive as ever, but there are fewer champions than usual. The Gwiazdowskis are out; ditto Ally and Tim. Perhaps they're all saving their verbal strength for the O. Henry next month. Isaac shows up toward the end of the warm-up, while Ariel announces her presence by doing a little dance with her pun partner that involves rubbing their butts together.

At the start of the first round, Jo Firestone calls out Punter S. Thompson with the rest of the names, and I go onstage to assume the position. The category is Barnyard Animals.

A million farm-bound images fight one another in my brain. It's an agricultural bloodbath. Goat. Boar. *Babe. Babe 2: Pig in the City.* Cow. Bessie. What were the names of Garfield's barnyard friends on *Garfield,* the animated series? The pig was Orson. Wait—was that a dig at the porcine girth of late-period Orson Welles? How did I not notice that until now?

Time is up criminally fast and I haven't written much down. This will be interesting.

If Looks Could Kale is up first, and I tune him out to think about what to do with the words on my board. The only pun I have written down is "free range rover" and if you gave a million monkeys a million typewriters to make those words funny, they'd throw feces at you and you would deserve it.

When it's my turn, I step forward, the most uncertain I've been on this stage yet.

"So, when I was a young lad growing up in Mos*cow,* I wrote a lot in my *dairy,*" I say. Here comes the soft parade of goodwill laughter that greets all but the most dour first puns of one's turn. Then I try out a "free range rover" pun, which is understandably dead on arrival.

"This is going okay," I say and earn a legit laugh because this is going barely okay at best. "I thought this round might be *gruff.* I was worried I'd *boar* you to death."

My voice is pitched low, in keeping with the self-deprecating pun style I've apparently cultivated. Surely this wasn't what Paul F. Tompkins and Randy Sklar had meant by selling a bad joke. All in all, it was better than if I'd curled into a fetal ball onstage and wept for two minutes, but not by much. I look down at my board and all that remains unused is the word *cock.* Great. I search for other barnyard words that might've escaped me but the glare of the crowd is too much to handle, so I wrap it up.

"All right, I hope I didn't *cock* this up too much," I say and retreat from the microphone like it's on fire.

Ariel's team is up next, and despite my disappointment I'm excited to see what they come up with for this topic.

"Did you hear about that one app horses use for making dinner reservations?" Ariel asks. "It's called *Open Stable.*"

"And when they do go out," her partner, Tracy, adds, "they get drunk on *Hen*nessey."

The two of them make it to the next round, as does If Looks Could Kale. I do not grab the third slot. My mind instead is awash with barnyard animal puns left unmade. Why didn't I make up something that would've "be*hooved*" me? Why didn't

I go to Eeyore or anyone really from *Charlotte's Web*? Punner's remorse is a motherfucker.

At the start of the next heat, pairs fan out across the crowded stage like a cotillion. What tonight lacks in regular champs, it makes up for in teams of first-timers. The category is Transportation. Isaac goes last and he absolutely murders.

"I fucking hate sedans and I hate SUVs," he says dramatically. "I'm sorry, I don't mean to be a *car-berater*."

Onstage, Jo covers her face as she laughs.

"I met a girl at the last Punderdome and we went home together," he says, arching a bushy eyebrow. "I used protection but we really went at it and, well, I burned rubber." Before the crowd can recover, he adds, "We were both really *tired* after that."

Just as his two minutes are up, Isaac throws in one more: "I rode out here in a family caravan tonight, so I had my nephew on one side and *Nissan* the other."

The heaven-shaking reception he gets helps explain why the champs keep coming back every month. Either they'll get in a friendly competition and push each other to be more creative, or they'll be the lone ringers in their heat as Isaac is here and stand out like a Krypton among Earthlings.

When Jo announces that the final topic for the first round is Baseball, a light storm of panic flashes across Sam's face. She shakes it off and starts writing immediately.

One after the other, almost everybody in this round uses *curveball* as a pun, and only one of them uses it to refer to an oddly shaped testicle. I finally understand what Jerzy told me so long ago about adhering to O. Henry rules at Punderdome—avoiding words like *curveball* that already mean something beyond their literal meaning, because they're technically not puns.

It's happening: I have begun to take puns too seriously.

Nikolai is on fire and is clearly headed for the next round. My eyes are on Sam, though, to see how she'll perform after eight months out of the game, and with a category she was actively dreading.

"I'm surprised there are so many groups of two here," she says. "Before tonight I've hardly ever seen a *double play.*"

The crowd roars and Sam barely reacts to it. She looks in control, a subtle smirk teasing way more puns to come. Something about her delivery makes you feel you're in good hands.

"I met a guy on a dating app for abusive people," she says in a far more chipper tone than the words suggest. "He was a designated hitter." The crowd is still laughing when she adds, "I set up some ground rules for us, though—one, two, three strikes you're out."

As Sam goes on, acting out bat swings and umpire signals where applicable, the cheering gets louder and louder. She destroys with puns on team names and then she closes with, "I don't know why you're at a pun competition, guys, you should go *home—run!*" It is such a simple pun, but she sounds joyful and self-aware, which makes it irresistible. Some guy in the front row yells "Boom!" as the room incinerates with laughter.

When the clap-o-meter comes out, Sam pulls her drop-crotch pants up over her arms and runs around like a wildebeest. Sam trained as a performer in a theater that stressed physicality, translating emotion and vulnerability into gesture and movement. It's part of what she brings to any stage she's on. She gets a 10 for this turn, and she earns it.

In the final round, Sam and Isaac end up facing off against each other, with Sam bouncing around like fireflies in a jar. Although it's a close call, in the end, she wins. Even if she knows next to nothing about baseball, she knows how to play with words, and she knows how to sell them. If her puns ever come across as sweaty, it's in a different way than Bob Belcher's. Bob pours a gallon of elbow grease into cooking up puns, and Sam puts the same amount into serving them.

# 10

## THE GRAFFITI CASTLE

There was a brief, flickering moment in which I thought a multiday drive from Brooklyn to Austin in a Prius full of punsters sounded like a blast. It was my most optimistic self: the guy who thinks maybe we won't need a dinner reservation, and the next postreunion Pixies album might be a real game changer.

That guy is almost always wrong.

Ally had been on the same page, championing a deep-crew road trip with the pluck of a Dallas Cowboys cheerleader. But the more I thought about it, the clearer I saw the reality of the situation. We'd be trapped in an aluminum pun box for days, our monochrome crew's Cracker Barrel puns getting more and more skin-crawly with every rest stop, like an actual barrel sluicing the stream of Niagara Falls, into word-twisty oblivion.

When I float the road trip idea past Tim, he asks if I'm serious. I pretend I was not.

We needed to decide on our travel plans soon, though. May was fast approaching, and with it the most intense week of punning imaginable. The week would commence with an especially high-caliber Punderdome to mark the show's fifth anniversary. Fred and Jo invited back every champ in town for an all-star tournament, leaving only a couple spots open for newbies like myself. The week would then culminate in the O. Henry Pun-Off, although it was still a mystery who'd actually get to compete. After that, who knew? Maybe the NSA would need help decrypting an all-pun communiqué from ISIS and call on us like a latter-day Scooby gang. Anything was possible.

Once the traction-less idea of a road trip was abandoned, we maneuvered through a labyrinth of e-mail threads to figure out a game plan. Everyone would be flying, not driving, but where would we stay? The Gwiazdowskis had a place lined up with their folks and their middle brother, Toby. Tim and his girlfriend, Meghan, would be holed up in a hotel on their own. But a cabal consisting of Ally, Nikolai, Isaac, Sam, Ariel, and myself were in for an airbnb, along with Max, the software engineer who tried to make a punning computer program. It only took one teeming Excel spreadsheet to home in on a spot. We were set.

After e-mailing with O. Henry's resident comptroller, I learned I was thirty-eighth on the wait list for Punslingers and twelfth for Punniest of Show. My chances of competing in the face-off portion of O. Henry were not so much circling the drain as having gone down it to live among the mole people, but the other event was potentially in reach. Still, it was hard to work up the antiprocrastination energy to put together a Punniest routine when I might not get to perform it. The event was two weeks away, and I hadn't done more than preliminary brainstorming.

All the recent O. Henrys were on YouTube in easily digestible chunks, so I'd seen loads of these routines by now. Like all pun-related happenings, they ran a gamut. Some were clever and powerfully delivered, but others were like supercuts of *CSI: Miami* one-liners: Detective Horatio Caine strolling around a morgue, making puns about each corpse one after the other. There are thirty-two total routines each year, so it takes something special to stand out. Ben Ziek's past triumphant topics include Alcohol and Cheese, the crowd-pleaser's crowd-pleasers. Perhaps mine didn't need to please everyone, though, as much as it just needed to be recognizable and packed with lots of syllabically varied cue words. I started running through possibilities. Dog Breeds seemed fun. Anybody who doesn't love dogs is a monster, so it was sure to get applause. But dogs as a topic might be too broad, and googling ideas for dog puns inevitably sent me down a k-hole of Unlikely Animal Friends. Soup was another prospect, but it was too narrow and thinking of so much soup at once made me want to barf. Another food idea, perhaps? What foods did I, a vegetarian, enjoy the most? Not vegetables, certainly, but there could be something to veggies as a topic. That might be *appealing*. So many choices, so much syllabic variance, so personal to me and my struggle to not eat bacon. Vegetables was a lush hanging garden of puns.

I called Jerzy and asked him what he thought of the idea.

"The rule for me is always pick a word set that's well known but not at the forefront of people's minds," he said. "And that's vegetables."

Jerzy was feeling pretty confident about his own routine, too. By doing a podcast for the past year, he and Jordan had been effectively writing a fresh Punniest of Show monologue each week. Although he won't cop to what his topic will be this year, Jerzy says he had written the first version of it ten months before, for an episode of the podcast. It was one of six options he forced his play development workshop to listen to and give feedback on. After deciding on an option, he'd since been in the rewriting and refining stage for months. By now he had it down not quite as cold as his Social Security number but more like an old anecdote you haven't told in a while.

Ziek, on the other hand, came up with the puns for his topic, which he politely declines to disclose, about a month ago and has only started crafting them into a story this past week.

The best Punniest of Show routines tend to have a narrative. With Jerzy's blessing on the topic of veggies, I felt ready to harvest a story from my crop. It didn't have to resemble in any way a good story, or even make sense, but the turns that resonated most always had a unifying theme beyond the topic. Ben Ziek considers romance the one thing everyone in the audience can relate to, so his stories were usually about dating. His cheese routine took the form of a literally cheesy love song, and his ode to alcohol told the tale of a barside wooing. Another champion who tended to focus on love is Big Poppa E, although his routines have historically explored just the physical act of love.

In a way, putting together a Punniest of Show routine is like writing a poem, and performing it onstage is like crushing it at a poetry slam. Big Poppa E is a three-time Def Poetry Jam challenger and he was once the reigning slam poet at O. Henry. He's also a gloriously ridiculous person. E is a white guy who sounds like a parody of a white guy imitating a black guy. He is also terminally horny. When he first decided to try his hand at O. Henry in 2006, E wrote a lewd routine filled with more double entendres than puns, and he ended up winning. The following years, his shtick became more divisive. No matter whether his topic was Candy Bars or Computers, it always turned into a tornado of dick and boob jokes, light on technical puns. Audiences loved these bawdy turns, but at least one judge always had a problem with them, and all it took was one low score to tank a turn. Eventually, these controversial turns ended up changing how the judges tally scores. E appealed to Gary Hallock to implement Olympics rules, which lop off the highest score and the lowest score and add up the remaining ones. Gary complied. The next year, though, when Big Poppa E turned in a clean routine about Harry Potter, audiences were less into it. That was the last time E competed at O. Henry.

Five years later, he tells me he's now ready to stage his O. Henry comeback this May.

I was nowhere near ready, though. I still had to come up with some kind of vegetable story. But nothing sounded blander than a story about vegetables. Any child who'd suffered the scourge of *VeggieTales* videos growing up could attest to that fact. But what if there was a twist? A pandering twist! I could tell a story about Austin's famous barbecue scene using all veggie puns. It might not be the most rad idea in the world, but it was *radish*. Now all I had to do was actually write the thing.

Coming up with hundreds of potential puns for a routine is standard operating procedure for some champs. They worked hard on shaping the idea and worked just as hard to memorize it so it would come in under the time limit, fully polished. One former winner, Austin-based troubadour Southpaw Jones, set his Punniest of Show routine to song, and he put at least as much effort into it as one of his actual songs. Last year he compiled puns in his Evernote app for weeks, before massaging them into sentences. Then he went through this list and rated each pun with one to three stars. Only the three-star puns survived. Southpaw then whittled a karaoke track down to two minutes and worked out where all the key changes would have to go, so he could meticulously fine-tune the timing. His performance that year was the Whitney Houston National Anthem of O. Henry turns. He blew everyone else away.

Southpaw says he isn't putting quite that much effort into his performance this year, though. But maybe he's just saying that, and he's actually putting in *even more* effort this time. After watching untold hours of O. Henry videos and talking to dozens of performers, I now just assumed feverish overpreparation until proven otherwise.


TONIGHT IS THE fifth anniversary all-star Punderdome. Only a few slots are up for grabs as far as nonchampions are concerned, and I have to hurry to claim one. I hustle down Fourth Avenue, beneath an ancient fort of green scaffolding attached to a crumbling tenement, past the odd luxury apartment. It's not hot out yet, New York only lightly threatening to inflict summer on us, but my body is in sweaty rebellion all the same. As I approach Littlefield, twin fleets of monstrously toned runners from the nearby CrossFit do drills down either side of Degraw Street. They dodge me like a swarm of bees before running back in the other direction, perhaps to do a thousand "burpees" on a tractor wheel. They've got their cult, and I've got mine.

Rekha is already on line, squatting with her back against the brick wall, wearing a hoodie with a rainbow stripe across it. It's the first time I've seen her since my first Punderdome, which she expertly won. She's been busy since, making funny videos for MTV, writing a spec pilot script, and touring with the Upright Citizens Brigade. Her Tuesdays have been spoken for in recent months, and she was lucky to make it tonight.

For a while, it's just us and a few other early birds on line.

Rekha is telling me about a trip she took to China recently with her dad when Sam walks over, her hair in a messy bun like the giant ribbon on a gift. Soon, Sam is recapping the night she and Ally helped Jerzy generate a pun name to replace the now-retired Jargon Slayer moniker. His plan is to use a different name each month, and Sam's favorite pick she'd put in contention is Hyper Bully. Mainly, though, she is excited about the shows she has coming up. She's cohosting *Previously On*, a *Mystery Science Theater 3000*–type thing Nikolai has just started booking every month, and she's starring in a fake TED Talk about the future (set in 1992), which she also wrote. Isaac is directing it.

Making a pun is mostly just making connections, so it figures that pun competitions end up connecting people. Punderdome has facilitated a lot of creative collaborations in its first five years. Many regulars have ended up making videos or shows with Jo Firestone, for instance, including both Sam and Rekha, and Tim used to host a storytelling show in his loftspace, where he invited lots of punsters. One of the greatest champions ever, Brian Agler, a.k.a. Punda Express, had a fateful meeting here one night with John Pollack, author of *The Pun Also Rises*. In addition to writing the definitive book on puns, Pollack is a former speechwriter for Bill Clinton, and he still has connections in the political sphere. While enjoying a postshow beer together, Brian mentioned to John that he was interested in speechwriting. It's not solely because Pollack was impressed by his new friend's punning ability that he reached out to a company in Washington, D.C., and put in a good word, but it didn't hurt. Brian's gain was Punderdome's loss, though. By accepting the job, he had to move to D.C., thus ending Punda Express's legendary run.

At the same moment, Tim rides by on a bicycle wearing a Canadian tuxedo, while Fred comes out to give away tonight's golden tickets. Sam and Rekha don't need one since they were officially summoned for this occasion. I happily accept mine.

"Are any of you part of that group that's going down to O. Henry?" Fred asks, absently tapping the remaining tickets at his side.

"We are, but I don't know if we're gonna actually compete," Sam says. "We're on the . . ."—finger quotes here—"wait list."

Fred gives us a paternal smile and waggles his eyebrows.

"Give 'em hell," he says and continues canvassing the line.

The rest of the O. Henry group gradually shows up once the bouncer starts letting us in. Ariel and Nikolai are talking with Sam, who is pantomiming climbing what looks to be a tree, for reasons I can't discern. Isaac is at the bar, laughing alongside Jordan and an older woman with blond-gray hair who has an Expecto Patronum tattoo on her arm. I join the group and after a few minutes ask Jordan if he's seen Jerzy yet.

"I haven't seen Jerzy in a month and a half," he says, coolly.

The last time the two were here, back in March, they'd lost as a team in the second round. Apparently, they'd both been extremely busy ever since, and no new episodes of *Punk Assed* have dropped in the meantime. Jordan has instead been auditioning for shows, and the burger joint he's putting together in Astoria, Flattopps, was finally set to launch within the next month. I decide not to ask about the fate of the podcast.

Usually some permutation of Punderdome's deep catalog of champions shows up, but tonight they're pretty much all here. Everyone I'd ever seen win and everyone I'd even heard about have all come out. The level of competition tonight is unprecedented. Whoever the human clap-o-meter is, they're going to need a bat's echolocational hearing in order to accurately call this one.

By the time Fred and Jo start their warm-up routine, almost the entire O. Henry crew is huddled off to the side of the stage. We could all probably recite Fred's puns verbatim at this point. In the past, I've spent this portion of the evening trying to turn mild dread into excitement, the most boring magical spell of all. (*Accio Xanax!*) Now I'm just curious to see what these people I've gotten to know over the past nine months are going to come up with. Everybody here puts their own unique tag on the antiquated architecture of language, like spraypainting the façade of some ornate building. By the end of the night, we'll turn this place into a graffiti castle.

"Now, how many people have been to a pun competition before?" Fred asks the crowd. "At some of these things, some individual, maybe a Ph.D. in linguistics or etymology evaluates the value of a pun and its philosophical underpinnings as an art. Who's been to one of those competitions before?"

The room is suddenly brimming with boos.

"Well, we don't do that shit around here, okay? We believe that we the people should decide!"

It sounds like shots fired at the O. Henry judges, maybe some leftover sour grapes from the time Gary Hallock came here last fall and took Punderdome to task right onstage. Maybe it's Fred trying to rile up everyone who is heading to Austin, his WWE mentality dividing the two competitions into heroes and heels. In any case, the crowd is responding to it with pep rally approval.

"We're gonna do something a little different this month," Fred says. "This is our freakin' fifth anniversary, we've got nothing but champions tonight, the best of the best, and we're gonna bring 'em all out onstage before we get started."

The applause is 90 percent supportive and 10 percent *fine but let's hurry this along, please.*

One by one, everyone clustered around me heads onstage in ascending order of how many times they've won. The comedian who bested Isaac in March on his first try, the Pundance Kid, leads the pack. Ariel and Nikolai are next, since they've only begun to win recently. Groan Up, an older gentleman whose puns are closest in spirit to the essence of a cymbal rimshot, heads onstage, too, glasses perched on his nose, pants hiked up to his belly button. Ally, Jordan, Sam, and Isaac join in and they're all clapping for one another and laughing like the cast call at the end of *Saturday Night Live.* As more champs emerge, the crowd sounds more impressed at the number of wins, cheers heightening into screams. Fred roars about Tim's ten victories as though no higher number could exist.

"This guy has changed names almost as much as he's won, which is sixteen times," Jo says. "I'm gonna bring him out by the name he has tonight: Quip Me, Baby, Bon Mot Time."

A shit-eating grin spreads across Jerzy's face as he strides onstage. When the applause settles, Jo and Fred bring Rekha out last. She has sixteen wins, too, adding fuel to the friendly rivalry between her and Jerzy for Punderdome supremacy. There have been a total of sixty Domes so far, and these two combined have won more than half of them.

"This is so cool for us, being up here with you guys; this is our family," Fred says, garnering a chorus of sitcom *aww*s.

"Now I'm gonna go down the line—everybody say whether you're single," Jo says, holding the microphone out.

Sentimentality defused, she shoos everyone offstage. The show is now underway.

The first category of the fifth anniversary show is Italian

Food. As the players start to write their puns, one of two twin sisters steps onstage to sing. Over the past few months, Punderdome has spawned a pair of official parodists who Weird Al Yankovize popular songs and make them about punning. While Wendy sings a version of "Piano Man" prepared especially for tonight, with a lot of the champs' names thrown in, another famous Punderdome sibling, Jordan, gently sways to the song as he writes.

Groan Up goes on first. "This place is packed," he says. "I never *sausage* a crowd."

The charm of this elder pun statesman's style is how shamelessly old-fashioned it is, a total throwback. Ariel is up next, and she gets things back on more of a modern track.

"This guy once took me to dinner and said '*meet balls*,'" she says, pointing below the belt with both hands like an aircraft marshal. "I said '*wine not*' . . . because I'm a *pro sicko*."

It's hard not to be won over by Ariel. She's so playful and so clearly enjoying herself, each pun followed by a barely suppressed laugh.

One of the few nonchamps besides me is Punrequited Love, a tall, amused-looking dude with scraggly hair in a ponytail poof, who's been at every show this year so far. Punrequited sounds exactly like he looks—like he just ingested a dense cloud of primo vape smoke. He starts off sluggish, but gets some laughs with a pun about his dream of cheating at award shows ("I think I could *rig a Tony*").

Jordan is up next, jostling his crimson jacket so the hood flies up over his head.

"This is gonna be quick because I *cannoli* think of a few puns," he says, making a face like he didn't just make a pun, like he's almost mad you suggested he did make a pun.

"A lot of women out here tonight," he notes, getting one sharp *woo!* from somewhere in the crowd. "The government wants to put its laws on your bodies," he says, raising his voice and pounding his fist into his palm. "And I don't want 'em to put their *laws-on-ya!*"

Huge, eardrum-eviscerating cheers. Jordan just ensured his place in the next round.

Over by the side of the stage, Ally, Jerzy, Sam, and I are all whispering Italian food puns to each other. ("How did scientists date anything before the *carbon era*?")

Now it's Rekha's turn. Jerzy straightens up to hear the first Punky Brewster puns since last October.

"I don't know if I can read this," she says, waving her board a little. "I *wrote teeny.*"

Jerzy smiles and claps like a rowdy Little League dad.

"My friends Rick and Kasha were supposed to be here tonight, and *Rick-oughtta* be here, but honestly: *fuck Kasha!*"

The rest of her turn is framed as an extended middle finger to the detested, imaginary Kasha. The crowd savors every second of it.

Despite Punrequited Love's enthusiastic pleading for applause, during which he chugs an entire beer and crushes the can against his head, Ariel, Jordan, and Rekha move forward.

Next is an appealingly broad category: Wild Animals.

Isaac is up first and he starts off with the typical Punder Enlightening scorched earth offensive—five or six puns just about bears in the first thirty seconds. They come so fast and unrelenting it feels like the audience never stops cheering.

"I'm not sure if just one pun about wild birds can win this round, but perhaps *two can*," he says. "But if I don't win, I don't give two *fox*."

This line absolutely obliterates the room. Isaac can't resist and takes an actual bow before rejoining the line.

"That was a perfect closer," I yell into Jerzy's ear.

"I've heard him do better," he yells back, shrugging.

The next team, 1–2 Punch, has a tight turn. It would definitely get them to the next round any other month. Words Nightmare and Forest Wittyker are still on deck, though, so they're not out of the woods yet.

Fred calls Ally next and she walks out, adjusting her glasses, little half smile, pulling at one sleeve of a cable-knit sweater.

"A lot of animals have been taken already, and I hope I don't *para-peat* too many," she says, making a face like she just splashed a pan of Bolognese sauce on a lady of affluence. The crowd laughs and Ally smiles.

"My *peer, Anna,* and I? We're actually the same cup size; we're *co-bra* partners."

Sam pumps her fist in the air next to me as cheers ring out. Ally finishes up with a couple of sex puns in a row, including the unavoidable riff about woodpeckers that was destined to emerge this round, and then she walks away from the mic.

When it's his turn, finally, Tim looks breathless from the first, sweaty and uncertain. He's going to have to dig deep to find unclaimed animals rather than put different spins on the Noah's Ark that has already trotted by. Tim never seems to use prompts other people have already uttered, though.

"There was something I was gonna *ox* you about," he says and makes a puzzled face. "Wait, *rhino* the answer. I was gonna *ox* you about this animal running around by the bar. I thought it was a dog but it was a meer*kat.*"

The crowd is on his side. It's classic Forest Wittyker; conversational rather than jokey, milking the cheesiness of each pun without hitting it too hard. It's his strongest showing I've witnessed. He, Ally, and Isaac move on to the next round.

In the final heat of the first round, Jo calls my name. It's a stacked lineup of five champions—and me. It's the most champs in any one round tonight, maybe ever—and also me. I glare at my whiteboard like if I look hard enough I'll see words beamed in from the future. The category is TV Shows.

Considering the approximately six million TV shows currently airing on every conceivable network, streaming service, and menswear blog, this should be a breeze. But for some reason, I have just as hard a time picking titles out as I do choosing something to watch. Damn you, infinite content!

Of all the shows that flash through my brain, it's impossible to explain why I write down the ones I do. Going obscure is a reliable strategy, but there's no reason to drag *John from Cincinnati* into this. Was *Buck Rogers* even a TV show? I don't know, but I definitely write it down. My pen doesn't stop moving until whichever pun twin is onstage stops singing.

Pundance Kid is up first; a big, squinty grin on his close-shaven, ovoid head. Although he's just as confident as last time, his turn is far weaker. Perhaps the level of gameplay tonight is so elevated it makes his puns look threadbare beneath his stand-up's delivery. Either way, he has way more misses than hits.

Sam is up next, and at first she fares no better, but then she gets revved up, and the room caves in to her.

"I like to put all my gnomes in a line, ever create some *lawn order*?" she asks and gets a deluge of cheers.

"Ever make a bunch of robot cameras in the sky fight and play a *game of drones*?" she asks, finding a groove with questions. The crowd stays with her the rest of her turn.

There's one pun I'm excited to do when Fred calls my name, but I can't open with it, so I start by following Sam's lead and asking a question: "*Wire* we all here?"

The audience laughs and my mind is scrambling. I need an answer for this. I look out and only see the bright light, something I was grateful for at first, for making me feel less nervous. It's like I'm telling puns to a Tinker Bell who either laughs or doesn't. Now I just feel disconnected from the crowd. Why *are* we here? My mind goes blank and I look beyond the light and see people waiting, but instead of going deeper into the panic, I just say the next dumb pun that pops in my head.

"We're here for *growing puns,*" I yell. There's a comedown from the previous laugh. It's a False Alert pun of the highest order. But surely better than had I stood there for a few more seconds not saying anything. Time to bring out the big guns.

"My only fear about going down on an alien from Melmac is *Alf all* on my face."

Once the words leave my lips, and the uncertain applause rolls in, I wonder why I thought this pun was going to kill. It's pretty gross, even by Punderdome standards. The audience doesn't love it, but I hear Sam howling over my shoulder, and I'm satisfied. I get through a few more puns and go out on a laugh.

When Nikolai is up, he uses *The Wire* as a prompt, too, but takes it another way.

"Have you seen that show where a guy just asks 'why?' over and over: *The Why-er?*"

He uses a bunch of equally silly puns, his voice zigzagging. For some reason, I notice he's wearing one red sock and one yellow sock, like hot dog condiments. At one point he looks down at the front row and asks, "Would you guys say you're *six feet under* me or maybe a little less?"

The crowd whoops so loud he might as well stop there.

Jerzy is up last, and he strides to the microphone looking eminently unruffled.

"*Cheers,*" he says, a self-fulfilling prophecy.

His turn is going typically well and as he gets further on a roll, his confidence transforms into cockiness.

"I feel like I have the benefit of going last because the guy who goes *farther knows best* what puns to do," he says, triggering a wave of awe from the audience.

"But I'm pretty sure I'm *gon' smoke* the competition," he says, closing his round out to colossal applause. Of course he's voted on, and so are Nikolai and Sam.

The next round is another tsunami of silliness. Jordan has the best turn in the first heat, but Isaac, Nikolai, Ariel, and Sam seem deadlocked to join him. After a seriously close applause audit, Nikolai gets the nod. If that choice was like deciding which of your childhood pets you love best, though, the next round is like choosing a favorite parent.

On the category of American Presidents, Rekha, Ally, Jerzy, and Tim push past any potential second-round brain drain and deliver epic sets. It's impossible to objectively choose a winner. Tonight's clap-o-meter, a guy named Eric, has the pensive look of a royal food taster as he probes the nuances between each person's respective applause. Jerzy is safe for sure (he got a 10), but either Rekha or Ally is tainted (both get 9.5s). It's down to a clap-off, and one that is just as difficult to differentiate as before, if not more so. Eric's read of the applause somehow rings as accurate, though. He picks Ally. Rekha looks briefly devastated, but catches herself, and claps for those moving on.

Fred and Jo should put Eric on salary and make him the clap-o-meter every month.

In the semifinals, the category is Brooklyn, and it's such a niche topic that everybody seems a little shook. They're all crouched into squats, boards against knees, brows deeply furrowed. Nikolai has scant ammunition, and he struggles with it. There's a familiar jokey desperation in Ally's voice, but it sounds less and less stagy as she goes along. She hasn't made it past the second round this year until now, and the existential crisis surrounding her career is still ongoing—it's hard to tell where her nervous act ends and reality begins. What probably puts the Gwiazdowski brothers over the top, beyond strong turns on a tough category, is that they both manage to make Lin-Manuel Miranda puns during the last gasp of *Hamilton*-mania's unshakable chokehold on New York in 2016.

"You found the brothers!" Jo yells to the clap-o-meter, when he selects the winners from behind a blindfold.

There are apparently a lot of *Punk Assed* listeners in the audience because the cheers are deafening. Jordan shadowboxes his way to the front of the stage, and then he and Jerzy grin at each other. They're about to do what they do every week on their podcast, and what they just may end up doing at O. Henry, if one of them manages to defeat Ben Ziek before the final round.

"Two minutes are on the clock," Fred says. "Your topic is Animals. Wild animals, domestic animals, barnyard animals, anything and everything—go!"

Jerzy speaks first, immediately. "I don't care who wins but I hope you laugh at *ocelet*."

"And to think," Jordan says in a withering voice. "I spent my whole childhood *fawn*ing over your puns."

Two minutes pass with nary a pause. Neither brother seems

to need a moment to think between turns. Everybody is screaming by the time Jo ends the round. A chant for two more minutes breaks out and she obliges.

"Two more minutes—same topic!"

The puns resume right away, blasting back and forth like British naval warfare. After nearly a minute, Jordan stumbles.

"What's an animal," he wonders aloud, laughing a little but also losing time. "Oh, hey, am I turning pale here, what's my *hue, man*?

Jerzy's face collapses into a crybaby pout. "'What's an animal? I can't think of a topic.'" he says, in a tantrum-like snit, "Quit *stallion*."

Jordan smiles and turns to face the crowd, a clump of hair in his eyes.

"The reason he started doing Punderdome was for *pussy!*" he says, yelling the last word. The entire room bursts into applause, especially the other champions, many of whom have gotten hit on at one point or another in this very room.

"Jerzy, *must 'tang* drive every one of your ambitions?"

Time is up. Everybody in Littlefield is shrieking.

"Can you imagine these guys at the dinner table?" Fred says, as the brothers hug.

Jordan is up first for the clap-o-meter. While he's mugging at the audience, Jerzy sits down on the edge of the stage, looks up at his younger brother, and starts clapping. Despite his encouragement, the audience is holding back just slightly. Jordan resurged spectacularly from a hard deficit, but it wasn't enough. Jerzy takes his seventeenth Punderdome.

It was possible that this group of punsters wouldn't all be together again for a while, so some of them confirm standing plans to go out for drinks afterward. The four female champions run onstage and take a picture in front of the glittering birthday banner that spells out "Punderdome." A lot of people threaten to hug Jo, who is an avowed nonhugger. Slowly, Littlefield empties, expelling its punsters out into the night, the words that made the crowd bay like wolves receding into the void.

# Finals

# 11

## MUTUALLY ASSURED PUN DESTRUCTION

The giant ornamental guitars at the airport are standing right where I remember them, doing their best to keep Austin weird. I walk past them, pick up my rental car, and head out.

It's Thursday afternoon and the O. Henry is in two days. At last check, I was number eight on the wait list for Punniest in Show and number thirty-two for Punslingers. I have more than a rough idea of how my carnivorous veggie routine will go if I get in, but it's nowhere near finished, let alone memorized. The plan is to work on it more tonight and tomorrow, if there's time. I've begun to accept the possibility that I won't be competing, though.

Our airbnb has been dubbed the Real World House, due to a miscommunication that made it seem as though the cast of *The Real World* stayed there one season. When I go to park my car, though, I see that the building itself is named Littlefield Lofts. We somehow picked the most Punderdome-friendly building in the heart of downtown Austin.

Max and Sam are already inside our space when I get there,

eating the complimentary tortilla chips and salsa the tenant left for us. The floor looks like mottled red clay dirt buffed to a shine. Its texture feels cool on my bare feet, which is a relief in the heat that comes with ditching New York for Texas in May. There are twin beds everywhere—two downstairs and three upstairs—along with a pullout couch Max has claimed for himself. In the middle of the living room is a painting that looks like a cartoon Johnny Depp in a fedora, with headphones the size of plump bagels and little ropy legs. I hate this painting.

Ally arrives next, followed by Nikolai, rounding out the Real World House early birds. Ariel and Isaac will arrive tomorrow, just before the annual pre–O. Henry banquet.

Immediately outside the apartment is a pizzeria with a sandwich board in its doorway that reads, "This is a sign you need pizza." In the search for a dinner spot, we pass a bar called Handlebar, with a black-and-white mural of O. Henry on its side. A Mazda 3 drives by with (.14) tacked on its logo, so it becomes the number for pi. A sign designed to look like the Jamaican flag announces Shangri-La's first annual Jerk Off, for fans of cooking with jerk seasoning. There's a laser tag place called Blazer Tag, catering either to stoners or perhaps just big fans of professorial outerwear. Puns are lurking everywhere we go. Everything is something else, the brown bag of a pun sneaking in the malt liquor of another meaning.

Together our shambling group roves through downtown, nearly getting run over by a flock of night bikers. In any group traveling together, there are always conflicting opinions on where to eat. Since we are in a town famous for Mexican food, though, and it happens to be Cinco de Mayo, everyone is in agreement. Soon enough, we're lounging in an art-filled cocina called Curra's, toasting with avocado margaritas.

"Here's to the puns that bring people together," Max says, a splat of salsa already in his tiny bird's nest beard.

"And the puns that drive everybody the fuck away," I add.

We clink glasses and drink up.

When the punning starts, it quickly becomes an indispensible part of the trip—the metro pass that gets you from place to place, the cruise buffet you return to again and again until you can't possibly take any more. Max throws out the topic of Weight Loss Movies while Nikolai is checking out the local Tinder situation and Ally and Sam discuss the possibility of going for a swim tomorrow. Suddenly we're engaged in a Hashtag War that never really goes away.

*"Lean Girls." "Ferris Bueller's Cheat Day Off." "Nutritional Treasure." "Love Handles, Actually." "Fasting and Furious."*

We may be tossing around puns just for practice, but I've practiced before and this feels like something else—a video game, a skating half-pipe, or to a lesser extent, a hacky sack. There's always another pun to do, another direction to take it in, and you want to keep going because maybe you'll be the one to come up with the best one. Everyone laughs at most of the puns, one or two go completely unacknowledged, but then there is usually one masterpiece that gets the most raucous cheers and shuts down the category. Coming up with the consensus pun feels as good as any amount of cheers from the crowd at Punderdome, as good as any retweet on Twitter. Literally anybody can do what we're doing, but not everybody can nail it.

These games follow us to coffee the next morning, when we wake up hungover, some of us wearing pastel sombreros with the brims ripped off. By the time we're caffeinated and piled into an SUV on the way to Barton Springs, the game has evolved to include mashup movie titles such as *The Sixth Sense and Sensibility* and *Don't Tell Mom the Babysitter's Dead Poets Society*. We spend some of the trip speculating on what these hybrid movies might turn out like, and everyone gets especially excited about the zombie aliens of *Independence Day of the Dead*.

At some point, the puns start becoming on-theme. When we hike through the forest at Barton Springs, the dry, cracked dirt resembling the floor of our airbnb loft, the titles turn to hiking: *8 Mile. You've Got Trail. Trekfest at Tiffany's*. We list off more and more, laughing as we avoid mud puddles and rogue branches to the face. When we get through the forest to the gorgeous springs, walking across shallow ridges that look like doughy bread loaves, we interrupt another group's dog party. The game then turns to dogs until the topic is exhausted and we strip down to swim in the water and shut up for a while.

The water is clear and cool, especially after our hike. Nobody says it out loud, but it's also a relief to stop making puns. This quiet afternoon reverie is necessary. In a few hours, our weird pun family is going to meet the weird pun family in Austin. If my previous visit was any indication, our mutually assured pun destruction was imminent.

WHEN WE GET to the pre–O. Henry banquet, everyone is thoroughly exhausted. Sunbaked, punned out, and caught beneath that extra bit of exhaustion at the trisecting point of a day with too many phases.

Despite the abundance of Domers in town already, only a handful of us walk into the restaurant together. Neither Jerzy nor Jordan has ever made it to this part of the event and they're not starting now. Isaac's flight was delayed. Tim and his girlfriend text to say they're going to a Flatbush Zombies concert instead, if anybody would like to come. They also ask if the place we're staying at is really called Littlefield, and how that is possible. Sam decides to take a nap and join Tim afterward. As groggy as the group that stumbles in is, everyone is eager to get a glimpse at who we're up against tomorrow.

In the back of a restaurant called Opal Divine's is a faded mint green bingo hall with what seems like hundreds of curtains. This is where our evening will unfold. There are anemic goateed dudes with Civil War hats, liver-spotted ladies with frazzled hair, a guy with a kimono over an Apple parody T-shirt that reads iPUN, and a general bouillabaisse of southern-fried individuals. The occasional younger man or woman mars the landscape of upper-middle age, like the disparate islands that make up higher double-digit tables at weddings. Indoor sunglasses abound. The pervasive style is Cool Dad, like if Harrison Ford's earring was in charge of casting a reboot of *Cheers.* Somebody in this room surely owned multiple Grateful Dead bootlegs from the Dick's Picks collection.

"It's very . . . generational in here," Max says quietly as we look for a place to sit.

Half a table is unoccupied in the back corner, and we head for it. There are printouts in front of every seat like placemats, and lots of people are hunched over, examining them.

As we take our seats, I spot Gary in a T-shirt version of the American flag button-up he wears to the Pun-Off every year, chatting with a guy dressed in full Elizabethan garb, including a purple jellyfish-shaped cap with a feather in it. There is probably a story behind this outfit, but it's not immediately obvious. Nearby, a freshly shorn Ben Ziek is holding court.

"That's the guy who wins basically every year," I tell Nikolai. "Jerzy's nemesis."

Nikolai looks Ben Ziek up and down. "We can take him," he concludes.

The printouts contain a series of pun riddles about entertainers: blank spaces for the number of letters and a clue to the person's identity. We all dig in right away. One by one, though, everyone's brows bunch up as it becomes clear that these clues were written in possibly 1986, with an eye toward the Golden Age of Hollywood. Many of the entertainers are dead, and there are references to Madonna and John Candy as hot new kids on the scene. Many of the clues make allusions to people none of us have ever heard of. Is it possible that the committee behind this dinner has been handing out the same game sheet for thirty years?

"I have a feeling it's not that we're stupid, but that this is," the chipmunk-cheeked brunette sitting next to me says, cheerfully, a southern twang in her voice.

Her name is Gracie Deegan, and this is not her first O. Henry. Not only has she been here before, she's won Punniest in Show before. This year, she's actually going to be a judge. It's her first time attending the banquet, though. So far, her review is that she ordered a margarita twenty minutes ago and it still hasn't arrived.

"Are y'all ready for tomorrow?" she asks.

"This guy's been practicing nonstop," Max says, pointing to me.

I want to explain that he's just joking, that I wish I'd practiced more or at the very least finished my routine by now, but I realize that's too much information.

"I'm just gonna go off the top of my head if I make it in," Nikolai says. I believe he could pull it off. Aside from winning at Punderdome, he's a compulsive storyteller who once finished a ninety-page feature screenplay in two days. He also founded improv clubs in middle school, high school, and college. If anyone can freestyle a Punniest of Show off the dome, it's Nikolai.

We fill Gracie in on our situation with the lottery, and she's surprised at how many people in our group didn't make it in. Her face lights up when we mention Jerzy, though. He's a friend of hers. Not only have they hung out at Pun-Offs past, but when she was visiting Brooklyn once, Jerzy invited her to Punderdome. Although she ended up getting shockingly snockered that night, she still managed to scrape a second-place finish, losing out to—who else?—Jerzy.

A clean-cut blond guy leans over from the other side of Gracie, introduces himself as Michael, and asks how we're feeling about tomorrow. Instead of repeating everything we just said, I say we're feeling pretty good and return the question.

"I'm feeling pretty good about it, too," he says with a slippery smile like maybe he feels really, really good about it. Before I can say anything back, Gary blows a whistle and bangs his keys against a bowling-ball-size bell like a gong.

"Welcome to the 2016 O. Henry Warm-Up and Punster of the Year dinner," Gary says. The reverb coming out of his microphone will not stop, but he continues talking, while a server fiddles with an amp nearby.

A young couple walks in and halts just beyond the threshold, taking the scene in. Their eyes convey a deep sense of alarm, the possibility that they've made an epic miscalculation. It's too late, though. Gary sees them and publicly directs them to the open seats near our table. They sit down and nod at us uncomfortably, like distant coworkers trapped in an elevator.

Gary goes on to give the history of this dinner. It's a tradition that started years ago as a hybrid of two other traditions. Every Friday, a month and a half before the Pun-Off, the Punsters United Nearly Yearly organization Gary founded would gather together to do weekly warm-up games, leading up to the big warm-up dinner the night before the O. Henry. Meanwhile, there used to be a dinner in Chicago honoring the Punster of the Year. These separate dinners eventually fused together into a gustatory hybrid.

"You all can try to figure out who the honoree is this year," Gary says, gesturing to the guy who is dressed like a high school Shakespeare play, "and the rest of us will remain ornery not honorary." His pun gets absolutely zero reaction.

In the background, the documentary *Pun-Smoke* is playing. Every now and then it syncs up so that a thirteen-years-younger Gary appears to be trapped in the wall, trying to send a message that present-day Gary is too busy punning to hear.

My phone buzzes and it's a group text from Isaac: "LITTLE-FIELD LOFTS???" None of us have fully gotten over this weird coincidence yet either.

"How many people are on the wait list and came down here on a great act of faith that they'll get into the Pun-Off?" Gary asks. "How many optimists do we have?"

Everyone in the Punderdome group's hands shoot up, except for Max, who never registered. Ally and I look each other in the eyes and share a silent happy-scream. Maybe we're going to slide into the O. Henry roster after all.

"Congratulations," Gary says. "You're going to play in our first round of pun games tonight."

Ally and I now roll our eyes. There's still a chance we'll get in, but I would've thought we'd know for sure by now.

Ben Ziek takes the microphone from Gary to MC the night's first game, which is titled Gyp-Parody, boldly sidestepping political correctness. The screen that was playing the movie abruptly shifts to a MacBook desktop, and then to the familiar stacked rows of blue boxes that make up a *Jeopardy!* board.

A punny game show could only be more inside Ben Ziek's wheelhouse if you could win it with a pile driver. This kind of game is exactly what he provides with his side business, only here he doesn't just squeeze puns into Alex Trebekian stage patter, but makes them part of the game itself. Ziek still hasn't heard back from the actual folks at *Jeopardy!* since passing the online test, but here he gets to play the game his way.

Up first at Gyp-Parody are me, Nikolai, and a stocky Austin punster named Marty. Although I've spoken to Ziek over the phone before, this is my first time meeting him. In person, he is friendly, charming, and a little intimidating.

"Joe, give me a number between one and Frisbee," he says.

"Um, four?"

"All right, go ahead and pick your topic."

I choose Fictional Characters. The clue is a folk hero who cries as he takes from the rich and gives to the poor. I'm almost inappropriately excited to know this one, restraining myself from blurting out celebratory expletives.

"Who is Sobbin' Hood?" I say, and Ziek congratulates me.

After this turn, I get one more correct answer. Then Nikolai jumps in when I don't realize the clumsy barber of Fleet Street is Sweeney *Clod*. From this point on, Nikolai just dominates, getting every single answer and completely shutting out poor Marty. It is not close at all.

"Don't let that goy push you around," a voice says, despite the fact that Nikolai is standing right next to me, and despite the fact that Texas is the last place I would've expected to receive misguided Jewish camaraderie. The voice belongs to a little old man nodding intently in the front row, wearing a baseball cap over some serious Willie Nelson hair. His name is Arlen, and he's up next, against Ariel and Ally, despite looking frail enough that the weight of the microphone pulling him down seems like a legitimate threat.

"I'm defending the honor of men!" Arlen says, and his two opponents sort of examine him like a thing in a museum.

This second round of Gyp-Parody is more abstract, with the players reverse engineering a setup from a phrase to turn it into a pun. Ally and Ariel are fully engaged, and back at the table Nikolai, Max, and I agree that a version of this game should wind up in Punderdome.

Ariel's eyes briefly appear to pop out of her head when one of the prompts is Cross Dresser, but punster Ariel prevails over LGBTQ activist Ariel and dings in to say, "What is a church interior decorator?"

"Any *chap'll* tell you that's a great answer," Ben Ziek says. He was born to host this game. Stage patter and puns practically drip from his pores as he keeps things moving.

"Who's Elmer Fudd's favorite Batman villain, by the way?" he asks. "*The Whittler.*"

Arlen stands by the entire time, grinning as though he either thinks he's ahead or has no idea what's going on.

Back at the table, Gracie begins telling me about her earliest O. Henry experiences.

"When I first went, there were maybe three women that year," she says. "It was surprising. I didn't realize punning was such an old man's game. But it's changing. It's getting younger and it's getting more female, too."

Apparently, Gary and David Gugenheim even pursued Gracie as an MC for Punslingers, which would've made her the first-ever female to do the job, but she declined. Being one of the Punniest of Show judges this year seemed like enough of a chance to get booed by the audience for making tough calls.

At one point, a lightly bearded guy with a huge smile squats near our end of the table and introduces himself as Jonah Spear. He's impressed that we've all come down from Brooklyn and wants to tell us about the pun competition he founded in San Francisco earlier this year. The Bay Area Pun-Off was apparently pulling 150 people each time out, just a few months in. It had taken off so quickly, Jonah was now planning to spin it off into a splinter cell: the New York Pun-Off.

"What?" Max says and gives Jonah a skeptical look. "What about Punderdome?"

"I know, I know," Jonah says, raising a placating hand. "Hey, there are a lot of plays in New York and nobody's like, 'You can't do a play, I'm already doing a play.'"

He has a point.

The pun games continue for the next hour or so, with different combinations of hosts and contestants. Eventually, Ariel is up against the Elizabethan-clad Punster of the Year in the final game. During the climactic round, when Ariel and the other players get forty seconds to write down a pun on the category of presidential candidates, Nikolai and Ally sing the *Friends* theme song to make her feel more at home. Ariel wins. It's not even close. Someone from Punderdome had won every single game tonight. Winning some warm-up pun games is far from the night's big honor, though.

The International Punster of the Year is the closest thing there is to becoming a made man in the pun Mafia (the punderworld). Last year, the honor went to Brian Oakley, who talked my ear off about pun strategy and knives when I was here a few months ago. Before that, it went to Steve Brooks, another retired former champion who is now active on the organizational committee and who will be one of the MCs tomorrow. Ben Ziek will clearly get the nod one day, too. Probably also Jerzy. This year, it's actually two punsters: Andy Balinsky, who has earned four medals over years of grinding it out at O. Henry, and Julie Balinsky, his wife, who organized this year's lottery system. These two were made for each other.

Several speeches follow, and then the award is finally offered, courtesy of prolific pun book author Stan Kegel, who has thick black glasses and an abruptly truncated Santa beard.

"Heh!" Gracie says, with a snort-laugh. I look over at her, my eyebrows raised, and she shrugs and repeats, "Kegel." I reach out and give her a very low high five.

Everybody from our group is looking at their phones by now. Ariel, Nikolai, and Ally are doing Snapchat face swaps, while Max and I text with Jerzy and Jordan, who are restless at the Best Western, wanting to meet up. I catch some of the older punsters looking at us with *well-I-never* bewilderment.

"Are you guys gonna go out on the town after this?" Gracie asks. "Can I tag along?"

"Of course!" Nikolai says, a bit too eagerly. A few minutes later, we start to slip out one by one. Just before I leave Opal Divine's, though, I remember something. One-half of the Punster of the Year duo, Julia, is in charge of the lottery system. Maybe she has an update on whether I've made it. I slink back inside, kneel beside her table, and congratulate her on tonight's honor.

"Thanks!" she says. "And thank you for coming down all the way from New York."

"I was also wondering," I say, cutting to business, "if you could check my current status on the wait list by any chance."

"There have been a lot of dropouts, so you might be in luck," she says, scrolling through her phone. I feel my stomach tighten as she continues to look.

Suddenly, Julia's eyes narrow.

"You're number two on the list!" she chirps. "I can't say for sure, but you should probably come prepared."

This is excellent news. It's all happening. If I get in, maybe Ally, Sam, Ariel, and Nikolai have a chance, too. Maybe this really will turn into the great Punderdome versus O. Henry showdown it's been shaping up to be all along.

# 12

## PUNNIEST OF SHOW

After leaving the banquet, we rescued the car-less Gwiazdowski brothers from the Best Western, where they were stuck with their parents, and went to a bar in the Rainey district called Craft Pride. It's a red wooden house adorned with Christmas lights and an overwhelming beer selection whose options, like Devil's Backbone and More Cowbell, sound like strains of weed or hot sauce. We settled into a wooden deck area, the ground covered in pebbles, with petrified tree stumps for tables.

"I hear you're one of us," Isaac says with a smile when he meets Gracie.

"Maybe y'all are like me," she says, scrunching up her nose.

Jordan is wearing dirty white jeans cut off at the shin, and he's letting Ariel and Ally draw on them with a Sharpie.

Inevitably, someone yells out "Beer Movies," priming the pun pump. Gracie looks confused a moment later as the beer-infused titles spew forth with volcanic force.

"How do you play?" she asks.

"Just say a pun," Jordan says.

And for the rest of the night, we all did.


I WAKE UP early on Saturday and take my laptop to Starbucks to finish writing my Punniest of Show routine, a narrative constructed almost entirely of vegetable puns. After spending a half hour on a pepper run that concludes with "*ah-been-near-yo* but now I wanna be *all-up-in-yo*," and deciding against it, I go out for some fresh air. It's time to memorize the gist of what I've come up with. If I make it into the competition, I'll figure out everything beyond the words—the inflection, tone, hand gestures, and whatever else—while I'm onstage. For now, I just need to walk around the empty morning streets of downtown Austin and recite my routine out loud like a total lunatic.

As it gets closer to noon, I head over to Brush Square, near the O. Henry Museum, where the Pun-Off will be held. The Pecan Street Festival is just setting up, with enterprising artists mounting rows of white tents like a shantytown outside of Voodoo Donuts, getting ready to unload their wares. Just in front of the museum, there's a Lone Star flag–colored trash barrel with DON'T MESS WITH TEXAS written on it, a reminder that Austin is like a tumor of coolness within a greater, Rick Perry–governed body. The registration table in the neighboring Susanna Dickinson Museum is inside a small room with wooden floors. A pair of bedpans sits atop the table, full of numbered stickers for each of the competitors. (The stickers for Punniest of Show are blue, and the ones for Punslingers are red.) At the end of the table sits Julia Balinsky, whom I approach and ask whether I've made it in.

"Well, you've climbed to number one on the wait list, but you're not quite there yet," she says. Her eyes are either apologetic or sympathetic, but it doesn't look good.

"Why don't you leave me your phone number, though," she adds, "so I can send you a message if we have another dropout?"

I jot down a row of digits and leave. On my way to go find food, I see Jerzy pacing near a merch table, unbuttoned chambray shirt flapping in the breeze, one arm in the air like a DJ hyping the crowd. His lips are moving, eyes focused intensely on nothing. Somehow, it feels more intimate and voyeuristic to see him in this state than if I'd caught him with his pants down. I hightail it out of there.

Jerzy is not alone, though. Many other dudes are pacing around, talking to themselves, as I cut through Brush Square. One guy with muttonchops and fat, rolled-up jean cuffs is reciting lines out of a notebook when he walks right into a tree. Without even looking up from his notes, he backs up slowly and then proceeds forward again, like a homonym-zombie.

Fiddle-heavy folk music drifts through the park, entertaining the crowd before the puns begin. The band is playing on a stage that rises only a couple feet off the ground, inside an enormous pavilion, the words *O. Henry Pun-Off* behind them in a font that looks like sloppy red paint set against a yellow oval. The old-school county fair ambiance is only broken by all the signs promoting the event's websites and Facebook pages and hashtags, though perhaps fairs have those now, too. Subaru-size speakers sit on either side of the band, with smaller siblings out in the crowd, slung over a huge tree branch like the trunk is wearing headphones. Reams of yellow police tape outline the entire tent area, perhaps someone's idea of a joke about a linguistic crime scene.

Ten minutes before the O. Henry begins, I'm alone at Juice-land, wolfing down a spicy quinoa wrap and banana peanut butter smoothie. When my phone buzzes, I'm sure it's Ally or Sam asking where I am, but it isn't. It's a text from Julia:

Come to the Registration Desk. You're in!

I'm already out the door and running before my half-finished quinoa wrap hits the bottom of the trash bin. I head back to the museum and fish out my number from one of those bedpans, thanking Julia profusely all the while.

"You're number two, though, and they're getting started right now," she says, "so you'd better get out there!"

I thank her over my shoulder as I run off toward the stage. On my way out of the museum, I see Arlen, the old guy from last night's banquet, and he sees me, too.

"Give 'em hell!" he bellows, as I hurry off. "Do it for the Jews!"

On my way toward the giant tent, I bump into Ariel and Nikolai. Ariel has a red sticker on her shirt—she made it into Punslingers! She notices my blue sticker at the same time, and we hug. Nikolai is, unfortunately, stickerless. I want to ask him if there's any hope, but since Gary Hallock and David Gugenheim have already taken the stage, I don't have time to chat. Nikolai points toward the area beneath the pavilion where they've set up base camp, and I give a thumbs-up as I speed off.

While I head toward the row of stageside porta-potties, old-guard champion Steve Brooks addresses the crowd. With his trim eggshell beard, he reminds me of a Scottish Terrier in a straw hat. Soon, he leads the crowd in a call-and-response definition of the word *pun:* "A pun is the humorous use of a word or words in such a way as to suggest different meanings or applications or words with the same sound but different meanings."

The O. Henry Pun-Off has officially begun.

The first contestant in Punniest of Show is a guy named Steven, who is fully decked out in athleisure wear, one sweatpant leg hiked up à la mid-'90s LL Cool J. His routine is about the joys of living in Austin, an early contender for Panderingest of Show. He calls Barton Springs, where we went swimming yesterday, an "Uber Pool," etc., and so forth. A minute and a half into his routine, the timekeeper blows an airhorn, and then at two minutes a bell dings. Steven has to stop. He had no idea that the six judges aren't necessarily all from Austin, and local-leaning routines are unofficially frowned upon. He gets wall-to-wall 7s, which are tallied Olympic style. With the highest and lowest scores lopped off, he gets a 28/40, setting a fairly low hurdle for everyone else to clear.

"Thank you, Steven, for being among the honorary cannon fodder today," Gary says.

This is maybe the last thing I want to hear just before my name. Cannon fodder. When Gary does announce me a moment later, I bolt onstage and take my sunglasses off to look out into the crowd. It's a totally different view than Punderdome, where you only see those bright lights. Here I can see everything. Vape pens galore—like shiny pan flutes at a Ren faire—bleach-faded jam band tees, picnic cheese sweating in the sun, a complete topography of balding heads like a chart of eclipse stages, rows and rows of collapsible tailgate chairs, bunched-up bodies glued to the ground, every kind of beard, every kind of sunglasses, more kinds of cargo shorts than denim scientists ever imagined. It is a lot to process.

The entire Punderdome crew screams when Gary introduces

me as the second cannon fodder of the day. But something about being called that brings me back to the moment onstage in Montreal, where I'd sort of thrown myself under a bus being driven by T.J. Miller. Back then, I'd felt too outclassed to say anything funny in my own defense. This time, circumstances had conspired to put me on early in the day, before the audience was acclimated to being punned at in the Texas heat. It was up to me to get this crowd on my side. I could be the cannon fodder, or I could push the *canon farther*. Ugh, I was incapable of not thinking in puns at this point. Lock me up and throw away the key.

"He came down here all the way from New York, so no pressure," David adds, smiling. "Start whenever you're ready."

I take a deep breath, and feel the heft of my routine under my tongue, like the words can't wait to come out. Let's do this.

"So, ordinarily I'm a vegetarian, but Austin is famous for its food, so here's a story about experimenting while I'm in town. I'll end this *corny* intro here *endive* right in."

Only the faintest chuckles ring out. They don't know whether they like me yet, but that's fine.

"*Olive oil* god's creatures, but I'm *arugula* guy and I don't *turnip* my nose at a meaty meal."

The crowd is laughing now, already, and it starts to feel more like Punderdome. Things go a little rocky for a while. I have a really forced way of mentioning "Mambo No. 5" crooner Lou Bega, just so I can say that something he did was "*rude-a Bega*," and that's when the microphone shorts out for the first time. The equipment is turning against me. What would it take for this to count as a technical foul so I can start over? It's too late for that, though. They've already heard the beginning, so I have to keep going and do the best I can. The microphone cuts out again right on a punch line about how the sound of chickens is my *bok joy,* but it gets a laugh anyway.

Just after a run of mushroom puns, the airhorn sounds. Shit, I'm not going to be able to get through this whole routine. I must have been talking like a meth-addled sportscaster while walking around downtown earlier, when it fit under two minutes. Well, either that or I'm talking like Harry Caray on elephant tranquilizers now. Either way: I'm not going to make it. I call an audible and skip over a whole section about tomatoes.

Toward the end, what I feared most would happen, happens. After I say "they *swish chard* order with another table," my mind goes completely blank. There's no time to summon the words back. I have to speak. Now! I repeat the Swiss chard line again, and this time I do magically recover the next line: "Stop *gherkin* us around."

The bell dings, but the words are rolling off my tongue like a freight train after recovering my thought, so I croak out one more line: "This is your *fennel* warning."

David gives me a look like I'm not very bright, the effect of which is lessened because he has snot coming out of his nose.

"It was a good routine, but unfortunately it didn't come in under two minutes," he says. "I'm afraid it doesn't count."

Oh man. What I had just done was like a slap in the face to everyone who was prepared but didn't make it on the list. All that effort and I wasn't going to even get a score.

"The judges should score it anyway, though," Gary adds, and I let out a deep breath.

The six judges sit in a row to the left of the stage, looking alert. A pigtailed, possibly hungover Gracie Deegan is slumped over on one end, and tiny Arlen is sitting in on the other side, making the judges' collective head height a bell curve. In the middle are circa 2016 Glenn Danzig, an anchorwoman, a guy who definitely owns a novelty apron for family barbecues, young George H. W. Bush, and the male half of the *American Gothic* painting. When Gary gives the go-ahead for them to score me, the numbers start flying up: 9, 8, 10, 9, 8, 9. It's a 35 out of 40, a very respectable score.

I did it. I came to this strange place, just barely made it into the competition, and did well. Maybe if I'd known for sure I'd be competing, I would've spent more time crafting the perfect routine. Maybe it couldn't have worked out any other way.

As I make my way to meet everyone else beneath the tent, I bump into Jerzy, which reminds me that while this moment may have been the pinnacle of my pun journey, it was still the very beginning of a long, fateful day for everyone else.

"I'm not up for a while, so I'm gonna take off," he says. "But I heard your turn and you did great—nines and tens!"

"Thanks!" I say. "Just out of curiosity, where *are* you going?"

"I'm just gonna go pace somewhere and maybe cut down my routine," he says.

And off he goes, like a knight clamoring to fortify the castle before attack. A few random people congratulate me as I walk through the crowd. Tim and Meghan clap me on the back on their way to the empanada truck. Finally, I stumble upon everybody beneath the tent, scattered around in an erratic grid, and they give me a hero's welcome—the first Punderdomer to perform at O. Henry this year. Then I settle in for the long haul.

Punniest of Show is a whirligig of wordplay, as one person after another gets up to perform. There are booming southern voices and gentle tepid testimony. Puns about football, puns about politics, puns in Spanish, each of the four kinds of Bad

Puns. Because they're only two minutes apiece, though, they mostly flow by at a brisk pace.

One thing that's inescapable is the sight of nervous people in cargo shorts. An hour in, it's clear there are as many ways to be nervous onstage as there are kinds of cargo shorts:

- There's the stiff-legged headlight deer; feral and cornered and soon to become taxidermy

- The incredible vanishing man, whose body is angled sideways to leave less exposed surface area

- The leaky faucet, with sweat expanding into shirt-archipelagos

- The heavy-breather, eyebrows arched heavenward like *why is this happening?*

- The stuttery, resting glitch face, like a worshipper trying to speak in tongues but grasping at straws

- The accidental pop-and-locker, with jerky, pelvic jitters, microphone shaking like a paint-mixer

- And the poker face pretender who ends up running off the stage like he's being chased by God

This is what happens when a rabble of introverts finally gets to do something they love and realizes they have to do it in front of a crowd. Some learn something new about themselves while others confirm something they've always feared.

The MCs onstage punctuate almost every routine with punny zingers. Sometimes it's pithy commentary on how the latest routine went over, and sometimes the MCs just see an opportunity for wordplay and can't resist. Many in the crowd share the exact same affliction, so the running commentary is welcome. It's part of what they're here for. Every now and then, though, the insatiable urge to make puns leads our hosts down a dark path. When a plucky young woman with apricot hair gives a spirited performance about pastries, the judges are surprisingly stingy with her score. As the low hum of booing begins, Gary clears his throat.

"The audience wants to curve your score," he says to the woman. "Can you show 'em your curves?"

Ariel and Ally look at each other like they each accidentally swallowed some rotten wasabi.

"Are you serious?" Ally says.

Onstage, the punster's glasses briefly levitate with rage, but she quickly recovers and walks away, stoic, giving the incoming performer an eye-contact-free high five. If the MCs feel any residual awkward tension from the moment, it doesn't show.

A lot of people turn up at the O. Henry dressed for the occasion. When Darren Walsh, winner of the UK Pun Championships, competed years ago, he performed in a chicken suit. Just last night, Andy Balinsky accepted his award for International Punster of the Year in full Shakespearean garb. Still, even after these previous signal flares, the pageantry and props of the O. Henry take me by surprise. Former champ Dav Wallace wears a sheriff's outfit to make an inspired stream of Color puns. An old man who looks like a Bill Plympton cartoon pulls out a stalk of broccoli and says, "Give me your money— it's a *broccoli rabe!*" A guy wearing a medieval leather doublet over a blousy shirt and steampunk boots slays with a *Game of Thrones* routine, while another dude decked out like a Spanish conquistador flounders with his saga of *Puns de Leon*. Andy Balinsky accentuates his outfit from last night with a pink tutu for a vanity-free turn combining Elizabethanspeak with dance puns—only too well, though. He crams in so many puns, so densely clustered together, that it sounds like pure madness, glittering gobbledygook. By the time he gets to the line "But *softshoe*, what *tights* do yonder *swingdow breakdances*," each word feels like an English professor tap dancing on my medulla oblongata.

The performer who gets the most mileage out of a costume, though, is Michael, the blond guy we met last night who'd been grinning like he had an ace up his sleeve. He did. Michael walks onstage in a crisp, tailored suit, carrying a tripod covered with a drop cloth. He turns away from the crowd and pulls out a tufty wig, like hay-colored cotton candy. Then he removes the cloth, revealing a mock campaign sign, dotted with bits of broccoli, which reads TURNIP: MAKE AMERICA GREEN AGAIN.

"Very exciting," says Sam, straightening up. She is not being sarcastic. This is by far the grandest entrance yet.

The one unifying element during all these months of punning is that everywhere I've been, everyone despises Donald Trump. Despite any differences between the Austin and Brooklyn crowd, he is something we can all agree upon. Trump has come up already as a brief punch line in at least three routines so far today, but this turn is totally dedicated to him—a stump speech using all vegetable puns. Vegetables have proven far more popular at the O. Henry than I had anticipated, by the way. Michael is the fourth person who puns on this topic, aside from me, the broccoli rob guy, and a woman in awesome white cowboy boots who had the inverted version of my routine, using meat puns to talk about being a vegan. Michael is committed to the bit, stomping around the stage in a contained frenzy, pointing at the crowd and saying things like, "We will not *cabbage-ulate* to *radish-al* Islam." When the judges scores go up, it's all 10s. We may have found our winner already. I don't see Jerzy around anywhere, but I imagine him pacing much faster now, his footsteps razing the grass and leaving grooves in the dirt.

As many routines as there are about vegetables, Michael's perfectly scored turn is one of only two dedicated to Trump. So far, that is. When Tim appears onstage, in calf-length jorts, tattoo of a sentient pineapple peering out beneath his shirtsleeve, the entire Brooklyn group greets him with supportive screams. Tim looks emboldened by the applause and right from go, he is charged up and talking faster than I've ever heard him speak. Tim's focus is trashing Trump, but there's no second angle— like, say, vegetables—so the puns are about anything and everything.

"Before he was in real estate, Trump was a pickle maker, but he couldn't master the art of the *dill*," Tim says, one arm in the air like *alas, poor Yorick*. "He had a side business selling terrible meat; it was a low-*steaks* operation. He also had a winery but he quit when he couldn't make America *grapes* again."

Tim rapidly rolls through food puns, Hitler puns, and currency puns—his blink-and-you'll-miss-it delivery a sharp contrast with Michael's sermon-like Trump routine, which he played to the cheap seats. The crowd is laughing the entire time, and Tim ends up with an almost perfect score, a 39. He looks satisfied as he leaves the stage to await his turn in Punslingers.

Although Jerzy is still nowhere in sight, Jordan has now joined our enclave beneath the tent, and he's brought the rest of his family with him. It turns out Jordan made it into Punslingers at the last minute, and so has the much-anticipated third Gwiazdowski brother. Toby Gwiazdowski has never been to O. Henry before, but he's a frequent champ at Pundemonium, the Punderdome equivalent in Milwaukee. If Jordan has a tendency to dress like a hipster vampire, and Jerzy looks like an art professor or magician, depending on the day, Toby looks more like a dad—probably because he is one. He has on a short-sleeve red gingham shirt and keeps his phone inside the breast pocket like Joaquin Phoenix in *Her*. Although he's the middle brother, Toby has the most receding hairline, and looks most like his dad, who in turn is wearing a KEEP CALM AND EAT PEROGI shirt, which is just incredibly on-brand for someone named Gwiazdowski. The family migrated here to meet us, but more important, to get an unobstructed view since Jerzy is almost up.

Every now and then, a pun is so bad, the crowd revolts beyond the level of mere groaning. They draw out the word *Awww* so that it projects something between scorn and sympathy, like "Why have you done this to us?" One brainy, grating routine about rhetorical devices is delivered so clumsily the audience looks shell-shocked by the time it's over. "I shouldn't let *e-pipha-me* off so much, but I believe *in-the-end-you-do*n't let me down about that," the punster says, with a ta-da flourish. When one of the judges holds up an 8, Isaac suggests that perhaps this judge is that punster's father.

Pun fatigue has set in. We haven't quite hit the three-hour mark yet, matching Punderdome length, but the repetition of watching one person after another march onstage and recite puns in a recursive loop requires far more spectator stamina.

By now, Nikolai is just yawning and swiping away on Tinder.

"It's all UT students," he says, when he catches me looking at his phone. "I'm maybe a bit past the point of dating college girls."

He's only a few years out of college himself, but every man must have a code. I think: Niko-*lay*, but dare not say it.

Tim and Meghan soon join our area in the tent, toting a twelve-pack of Lone Star and a flask of whiskey.

"Jo Firestone told me the most important thing is to bring a blanket and lots of beer," Tim says, still flush from his victorious turn onstage.

Nearly everybody grabs a Lone Star.

Jerzy suddenly emerges from wherever he'd been practicing and waits in the wings with Ben Ziek. Jerzy is pointing at the performer currently onstage, and Ziek is nodding along, as though the two are appraising a painting. When this punster is finished, Gary Hallock and Steve Brooks take great care to mention that he braved a trip to the O. Henry all the way from New Jersey.

"'Speaking of Jersey . . .'" Ally says in a dopey voice.

"Speaking of Jersey . . ." Gary says a second later, prophecy fulfilled. Gary is then briefly drowned out by all the clapping and whooping from the Punderdome group and Jerzy's family. Much of his last year has all been leading up to this moment.

Jerzy looks too focused to inhale oxygen. He is a slingshot stretched tight, a wheezy teakettle, a starved Doberman who smells steak on the other side of the door. He keeps touching his hair and nodding while the MCs introduce him.

"How many times is this for you?" David asks.

"This is my fourth time."

"May the *fourth* be with you," Gary says, before adding, "and sometimes *metaphors* be with you."

A hero in the audience yells out "Don't stop!" and chortles like a mall teenager.

It is with the squelch of microphone feedback that Jerzy launches into his opening line, which explains the premise of this routine: "Stop the wedding! I just walked through all fifty countries in Asia to be here. Actually, *I ran*."

He hits the ground flying, cranked up to an 11 from the moment he opens his mouth. It feels like overkill at first, you can practically taste how bad he wants to win. Jerzy is trying to bludgeon the crowd into submission through intellect and sheer force of will. Every word is deliberate and necessary, though, with no filler whatsoever. His hands pulsate in the air like hummingbird wings—*stay with me, watch what I'm doing*—as he finds a sweet spot between cerebral and silly, and soars higher and higher.

"I been in a *malays*-since *ya* left," he yells. "But I think the jig isn't up for me, because I think *tajikistan*ding up for what you believe in. *Afghanistan* up for myself. Be-*kazakhstan* here knowing I don't stand alone, that's what gives me the *kyrgyzstan*. I look as John stands. I look *uzbekistan*s. And John as you're by Becky and Becky as you're by John, now there *Armenia* us, the whole *pakistan*ding up. *Yeah-men!*"

The crowd noise is a rumbly orchestra of goofballs going gaga. Steve and Gary onstage look riveted, grinning ear to ear. Today is their Christmas.

Jerzy loses his place for an instant, shaking his head, eyes wide—ninety-second airhorn blowing as he stutters. Then he inhales deeply and says, "Listen, here's what I'm trying to say, baby." Text merges with subtext and he's talking directly to the crowd, not his fake international lover. *Disregard that flub, the closer is coming.*

Just before the bell dings, he squeezes in his final line: "I can't go *Lebanon* without you, because what we have *Is-rael!*"

The cheers that follow are Yankee Stadium–level, far surpassing Punderdome, and they go on and on. Jerzy lets out a breath and clutches his stomach like he's going to collapse. His score is 10s all across the board.

"We could've saved a lot of time if he'd gone first," Steve Brooks says.

Max looks at me and we both just shake our heads. Jerzy is on another level. His is the second perfect score of the day, though, so the trophy doesn't have his name engraved on it yet.

As the next performer takes the stage and launches into a resoundingly average punologue, some people get up to stretch their legs. The momentum of Jerzy's turn quickly dissipates and is replaced by something between amusement and indifference. There's still plenty of crosstalk going on when former champ Southpaw Jones takes the stage next, so the audience is taken aback when he starts to crush. Southpaw is equally as passionate as Jerzy, but more chipper. His topic is Birds and he manages to cram in dozens of avian puns as gently and fluidly as one of those drinking bird toys.

"*Beek* kind to me, don't *thrush* to judgment, I'm not *robin* anyone, *hawking* anything, *talon tails* out of school, *ducking* responsibilities or *emu*lating anyone," he says, getting a huge laugh. When he's finished, he takes a knee, looking just as drained as Jerzy did after his turn. The crowd response is similar, too. It's the third perfect score of the day, something completely unprecedented at O. Henry.

The judges aren't pushovers, either. Unlike the Punderdome clap-o-meters, these guys don't shy away from giving 5s and 6s. They won't candy-coat contestants' scores for the sake of self-esteem, and when they're turned off, they let it be known. The judge who looks like the *American Gothic* farmer, for instance, always seems at least a little aghast, especially during the occasional sex pun. The O. Henry is a family-friendly event, light on racy material. We make it almost all the way to the end of Punniest of Show, for instance, before getting a seriously filthy entry. Then a young guy with a lumberjack beard starts with a pun about handjobs, and gets way raunchier from there.

"I had thought about making pasta but I'm very particular about it," he says, flatly, "because I'm an *anal linguini-ist*."

Before today, the O. Henry has never seen three perfect scores before, nor had it ever heard a pun about eating ass. It's a historic day.

The judges give this performer lots of 6s and 8s, but Gracie holds up both a 6 and a 9. None of the other judges seem aware why folks are pointing toward them and laughing.

In an unfortunate case of timing, the star slam poet Big Poppa E is up next, his long-awaited return to the O. Henry stage after five years away. The man born as Eirik Ott has won here before with his bawdy routines, partly because they were such a break from all the PG-rated material preceding them. When everybody in the crowd has just heard a guy make a pasta-based analingus pun, though, they just may be too desensitized to perk up much for a guy talking about going to a dog park with "my big fat wiener hanging out." It's like being offered dessert after pancakes.

Big Poppa E—diminutive, bushy bearded, clutching a Moleskine—gets some laughs, but his face buzzes with awareness that he's not killing. When the judges score him, he gets all 8s and 9s. Afterward, E shuffles offstage and over to a beach blanket beneath the pavilion, looking deflated. His wife puts a tender hand on his thigh, smiling warmly. There's always next year. Maybe not, though.

When Ben Ziek is finally up, he takes a moment before his turn to address the crowd.

"Can I just say really quick, to everyone's performances so far: you guys are amazing, you really raised the bar."

As the crowd claps, seconding Ziek's praise, Gary adds, "No *pander* intended," and the cheering tapers off.

Ziek's primary forte is Punslingers—he's won it four out of the past six years—but he's also won Punniest of Show twice. His turn today makes it obvious why. Although Ziek has the build of a certain kind of wrestling heel, he's surprisingly limber on his feet, miming his way through a routine that's all about dancing. Andy Balinsky may have had the same topic earlier, but Ziek puts his own unique spin on it, and his puns have the same effortlessly dense quality as Southpaw Jones's.

"I'm in a two-step program," he says near the end. "Will it *twerk*? *Hula* hell knows."

It's an impressive turn, but after three perfect scores already, the ceiling for impressing the crowd is high. The judges give Ziek a 37, and he betrays no disappointment with it. He still has another chance to win, with Punslingers, but from his unruffled demeanor, winning appears not to be a concern.

After all thirty-two contestants have finished, Gary summons Jerzy, Southpaw, and Michael to the stage for a clap-off to decide the winner. In place of the audience-pleasing and body-gyrating Punderdome version, Gary instructs each of them to perform thirty seconds of their routines again. Michael is up first, still wearing a full suit and flouncy Trump wig. He launches right back into the middle of his routine, leaning into a campaign speech voice. Without the momentum leading up to this excerpt, though, it falls a little flat. Jerzy dials down the enthusiasm a notch during his turn—the emphasis on clarity, rather than beating the clock—and the audience laughs in kind. Southpaw sounds just as exuberant as before, but he loses his place toward the end and gives up, yelling, "That's all I have!"

When David asks the crowd to cheer for Michael, the Trump surrogate raises up his giant blue campaign sign—MAKE AMERICA GREEN AGAIN—and there's a note of reserve in response. Everybody is holding back, but for whom?

Jerzy's face is at war with itself in this moment before his applause is to be weighed like a prize fish. He's smiling, but it's a trembly smile. Nobody looks as worried as someone trying hard not to look worried. But then Jerzy steps forward and the tremble is gone as the crowd reacts to him. Everybody in the Punderdome group is on their feet, dumbing out, and when I look over the crowd, several people in the sprawling field behind O. Henry's house are standing up, too, overhead clapping like a Springsteen audience during "Born to Run." Onstage, Jerzy whips out his phone and takes a picture of this ovation, which keeps going even after the airhorn blows to end it.

"Sounds like somebody has some special delegates," David says, gesturing toward where we're sitting.

Southpaw draws more crowd-love than Michael did, but the audience seems to be holding back again. The people have spoken, and the MCs recognize it immediately.

"I think we have it decided," David says, looking across the stage at Gary and nodding. "In third place: Michael Kohl."

Jerzy betrays no worry from where he stands onstage.

"Second place: Southpaw Jones," David says.

All the Punderdomers are on our feet again, cheering. Jerzy has just won Punniest of Show at the O. Henry for the second time. Of course, there's still the matter of Punslingers, the only trophy Jerzy hasn't won yet. He came here to retrieve it, and he's about to get his chance. However, first he's going to have to get past Ben Ziek or possibly Isaac, Ariel, either of his brothers, or any of the other contenders. Even though Jerzy is already exultant, pumping his fist onstage, the real battle is about to begin.

# 13

## PUNSLINGERS

The first round of Punslingers is endless. In what humans call *time*, it takes less than two hours. Considering we'd already sat through hours of puns beforehand, though, it feels more like the interminable unfolding in which yarn is knitted into fabric and sewn into clothes and those clothes go out of style.

It smells like sizzling pork sandwiches and gooey Mexican food under the tent. The crowd sits on unfurled blankets and towels, beside coffin-size coolers, shifting positions regularly like they're stuck on pointy twigs. Frat bros, dungeon masters, and mommy bloggers all share the same facial expression. It's anticipation of amusement—an agape-mouth-with-flies-moving-in-and-out kind of look. There's also the occasional satisfied grin of someone memorizing a pun to repeat later.

"They don't have to be good" is the watchword of Punslingers, a constant mantra for when someone drops a pun so bad you can't even believe it. We don't have to wait very long to hear it. Steve Brooks says it after Hannah Nelson's very first pun in the very first face-off, on the subject of Farming—"A lot of *fakers* out here. You know, like 'acres'?"—just before Ben Ziek systematically dismantles her.

"I like to *pig* out on food," Hannah says, sunburned beneath a floral shift dress.

"Me, too," Ziek replies. "And then I like to take a big *crop*."

He returns every pun with ping-pong topspin and a conversational flourish, and he's gently funny. The crowd swoons.

"I like to go to the *old McDonald's* to get a burger," Hannah offers.

"I'm much *loft*ier than that," Ziek shoots back.

Well, they're not always funny. But they keep coming, unrelentingly, until Hannah fouls out a few minutes later.

Punslingers works much differently than the duels that end Punderdome each month. There's no time limit, which allows more sure-footed opponents like Ziek to wage a war of attrition. Because the first round has plenty of first-timers, the MCs give contestants a chance to fix puns that are not puns, such as Hannah's offering, "I recently bought a *trucker* hat," which baffles everyone. Each time a contestant repeats a pun their opponent has already used, he or she takes a strike, which is noted on a number flipboard center stage. The crowd has a way of keeping the MCs on their toes when a pun has already been used: they yell out "Used!" over and over until the strike is registered. Three strikes and you're out. Don't come up with a pun after a five-count and you're out. When it's Brian Oakley doing the count, he brings his arm forward like a fly fisherman, making numbers with his fingers. His eyes betray a solemn respect for upholding justice in this duty.

Sometimes the MCs' edicts seem rather arbitrary. In an early round on Space Travel, they put the kibosh on all fictional space vehicles after the players pun on *Millennium Falcon* and Chewbacca, which seems odd. They could've just specifically outlawed *Star Wars* puns and left open intellectual property such as *Moonraker,* the *Enterprise,* and *Event Horizon.* Considering how long some of these rounds go on for, though, I guess I should thank them.

In order to preemptively fend off strikes, almost every player ends up explaining their puns right after saying them. Sometimes they do it in the meek tone of a person trying to get out of a parking ticket. Other times, it's with the authoritarian steamroller style of Bill O'Reilly warding off any counterarguments. The funny puns don't need an explanation ninety-nine times out of one hundred, and when the unfunny ones are explained, they often go from nonsensical to depressing. The lone bright spot of this excessive explanation comes early on when the Space Travel category prompts one woman to say, "You'd better *lance* that wound you're getting with all these sharp puns. You know, like Lance Armstrong?" It's not every day you see a person learn that the first man to walk on the moon did not also win the Tour de France or lose a testicle.

After playing the Movie Title game all weekend, the entire Punderdome group perks up when Movie Titles is announced as a topic in round one. It's the sheriff from earlier in the day, improv master Dav Wallace, against the sex lumberjack whom Gracie rated a "69." Several of their puns are decent, but after all the movie titles that had us cracking up over the past few days, these mostly sound like unsexy porn parodies. It reminded me of the pun-titled *Air Bud* series, a spirited collection of films about a sporty dog that includes *Golden Receiver, Seventh Inning Fetch,* and *Air Bud Spikes Back.*

"This Japanese emperor slapped a guy from Japan, it was the Empire Strikes *Vlad*," says the bearded guy who, mere hours ago, on this very stage, made a pun about rimjobs.

"'Vlad' doesn't even sound like 'Back,'" Sam says in a huff.

"And why was he Japanese?" I ask. "How many Japanese Vlads are there?"

Later, the same guy simply says, "It was Lucky Number *Seven*," and explains that this is a pun on the justly forgotten Josh Hartnett film *Lucky Number Slevin*. It was a pun on a pun title, turned back into a nonpun, like if someone laundered drug money to buy more drugs.

I grope around desperately for one of Tim's beers and promise to pick up the next twelve-pack.

Some of the players have a clear command of strategy. They know to phrase puns in the form of questions, which psychologically pushes their opponents to respond quicker than they otherwise might have. This maneuver also helps if your pun is weak and possibly strikable, because if the other person starts responding before the judges move to strike it, that person has officially accepted the pun. The question strategy can backfire for rookies, though. Heavy hitters like Ziek and Jerzy can reflexively answer any question in pun form, so you'd better be ready to have a whole conversation if you start up with them.

Some of the other players don't seem to know what they're doing at all, as though they were on the way to go pick up some Cracklin' Oat Bran and accidentally ended up onstage.

Jordan Gwiazdowski's challenger is an elder hippie in a headband who looks like he's been lying low in Hawaii since the heat cracked down on the Manson family.

"I feel like a bird on a wire," he opines, on the category of Birds.

"Now that's an example of a pun that's not a pun," Steve Brooks says. "That's a cliché."

Jordan has been practicing for an entire year. He deserves a more formidable opponent than this sweet old dude. It's obvious that Jordan will win, but he's a graceful winner. At one point, he gestures to his clearly outplayed opponent and says, "Some of you can't make puns but this *fella can.*"

The adorable old guy stares straight ahead in silence for a moment. Then he says, "I'll fly away," before skedaddling off.

Very few other rounds end as quickly. In one, a rangy hair metal wizard defeats Arlen, who looks like a wizard who has retired in Fort Lauderdale, with a single pun. Tim Donnelly wins his round on Railroads in practically no time, and Toby Gwiazdowski makes short work of his challenger as well.

"He's a Gwiazdowski," Sam declares. "It's in his blood."

Isaac and Jerzy have slightly longer first rounds, but cakewalks they are not. Isaac's opponent turns out to be the male half of the young couple that booked it out of the banquet the previous night, shortly after they arrived. He's a sporty bro in shoes with fluorescent laces, who looks like he just got back from the gym. It seems to be kismet in his favor that the category is Exercise. Early on, though, MC Brian Oakley gets up to a four-count waiting for the guy to make a pun, and all he comes up with is, "I'll just have to muscle through this one."

Steve Brooks shakes his head and frowns.

"'Muscle through' is not a pun," he says. "Can you make a pun on the word *muscle*?"

Isaac's opponent, who is probably at this moment on the paleo diet, puts his hands on his hips.

"I was trying to fish for clams the other day, but all I caught was a *muscle*?"

The line is met with strictly participation trophy laughter.

"If you can't think of a muscle pun the first time, just *weight* for it," Isaac says, and swaggers a few steps back to his spot. He looks like he has this locked up, and eventually he does.

Everybody from Brooklyn—well buzzed by now—gasps when Jerzy's category is revealed. It's the American Civil War, the kind of topic that would probably never come up at Punderdome. Jerzy looks totally unfazed, though. He's prepared for this sort of thing by now. But the guy in baggy dad jeans whom he's up against seems ready, too.

"Ever go to Pamplona and see the *Bull Run*?" he asks, eyes downcast beneath his glasses.

"Yeah, you're doing a good job *Lincoln* these words together," Jerzy says.

"*Sumpter* is better than nothing."

"*Sher-man*," Jerzy replies.

The crowd wails, and Jerzy's opponent smiles begrudgingly. They volley back and forth another few minutes, until the guy stumbles responding to a cannonball pun. He's out.

Ariel is up next. She hits the stage looking cheerful in a backwards bike messenger cap with pastel flowers. Our whole group winces, though, when her category is announced as Country Music. Max, Sam, Ally, and I look at one another searchingly, as though one of us might have intel on Ariel's ties to the Nashville music scene. No one wants to admit to stereotyping country music fans, but Ariel just doesn't seem like one of them.

She starts out making puns on top-tier female country stars. She does Reba McEntire, Shania Twain, and Taylor Swift from the days before Kanye almost let her finish. Then she hits a snag.

"Of *chords* my next pun is gonna be about music," she says.

"The category is Country Music, not Musical Instruments or Musical Terms," Brian says, nearly as stern as Walter in *The Big Lebowski* yelling "Over the line!" on a tiny bowling infraction. Her pun was definitely a stretch, but the MCs have let worse slide already today. The crowd collectively sucks its teeth. Ariel puts her hands on her sides—smiling but indignant.

"Arms akimbo, really?" Brian says.

"Ugh, she's allowed to be akimbo," Ally says, rolling her eyes. "I can't, with this."

Just when Ariel looks like she's about to go down, she says, "I like to cook on the border of two states: I *wok* the line."

Everybody in the crowd cheers, and so does Brian Oakley, despite his harshness moments ago. Ariel's opponent, a tall, Brillo-haired guy in glasses, sends a puzzling Johnny Cash pun right back in her direction.

"I shot a man in the *peen-o* just to watch him dry," he says, shrugging.

"I, uh," Ariel says, fingers flexing, as if trying to pluck a pun out of the ether. "I'm gonna use '*wok* the line' again so I can get a strike and have more time."

Brian flips over the first strike sign and starts doing a five-count on his hands. Even though she bought herself a few more seconds, though, Ariel is now just staring at his hands, pursed lips beneath a quivering brow. Her time has run out.

Ariel is composed enough to reach over and shake her challenger's hand before scurrying off the stage. Sam immediately gets up from the blanket and runs after her.

Due to a clerical error, Janani Krishnan-Jha, a silky-haired high school senior, has to battle two opponents in one anomalous three-way round. She's up against an unhappy-looking older man with eerily smooth shins, and the cocky older brother from a British coming-of-age movie about soccer hooligans. This quickly becomes the tensest contest of the day so far.

The MCs seem to be actively trying to avoid causing discomfort for a person of Indian heritage. They go a little overboard apologizing about mangling Janani's name, but at least they're trying. However, this is all the respect they grant her, as Janani seems to get challenged for her puns more than her male opponents on the topic of Moviemaking. The older player makes two conflicting puns on the word *her*—"I had to *direct her* up here," and "I had to *trail her* up here"—and the judges let it slide. Meanwhile, Janani has to emphatically defend several of her puns.

Moments after Brian and David announce that proper names like George Lu-*cuss* are no longer viable, Janani says she had a friend named Elizabeth Donatto whom she calls "*Ellie D.*" Even though the soccer hooligan accepts the pun by starting his next turn, David charges toward the flipboard.

"You just said a proper name; that's a strike," he says.

"I believe the pun was on LED," Janani says, calmly.

Back in the crowd, we're screaming our lungs out to defend Janani as though she were our collective love child. Eventually, David overturns the strike. It feels like being on the ground floor of the least consequential civil rights battle in years.

"I can't believe this is *reel*," Janani says on her next turn, perhaps an indirect wink to her supporters.

In the end, she outlasts both competitors, ironically when Manchester United accidentally reuses the other guy's "*trail her*" pun and trails Janani permanently.

By the end of round one, the crowd's spirit is broken. Laughs and applause are far scarcer than during Punniest of Show, people coming most alive in the face of possible injustice. It gets so quiet sometimes, you can hear birdsong in the tent and the sound of Tupperware unfastening. Meghan sums up the general sentiment succinctly: "I no longer care what anybody onstage has to say." Then she passes me a flask of whiskey.

As round two gets going, though, a new charge crackles in the air. The serious threats start to play each other in heats that feel more like trench warfare.

Dav Wallace, who has been an improv performer since 1997, proves a worthy adversary for Jordan Gwiazdowski. The two spar back and forth on Fairy Tales in a friendly grudge match. Jordan's puns have a little more panache at first—the difference between "Let's *beast*-erious" and "Sleeping *booty*"—but Dav keeps them coming, forcing Jordan into survival mode. The inner turmoil of wanting to win with style, and needing to simply outlast, is written in the creases of Jordan's forehead. After a while, though, Dav starts to lose stamina.

"This is getting *grimm*," he says, ten minutes in.

After squeaking by on a few almost strikes, like "This is the last *draw*" as a pun on the concept of straw in fairy tales, Dav goes out by reusing a Rapunzel pun.

Jordan had the misfortune of going up against Ben Ziek in the first round the previous year, and his first opponent today wasn't a challenge at all. This bout with Dav Wallace is the first time he's truly proven his mettle at the O. Henry.

Isaac is up next, facing off against Jerry Yan, who barely won his first at-bat.

"He's got this one sewn up," I tell Jordan.

"I wouldn't be too sure," he says. "Toby and this guy are always bumping up against each other at Pundamonium."

Apparently, this young man with a perfectly symmetrical bowl cut is the Ben Ziek to Toby's Jerzy. Or something like that. The topic of his round with Isaac is Pregnancy, which seems like it can end no other way than "creepily." I brace myself for puns about placenta.

"Baby Jesus didn't *diaper* your sins," Jerry says, and we're off to the races.

"There might be a baby in your gaze, sir, you have *fertile-eyes*," Isaac says, coquettishly, a hand on the side of his face.

The two remain on even keel for a long while, but then, for the first time I've ever seen, Isaac starts to sweat. Even when he lost in March to the Pundance Kid, he remained cool as an Otter Pop the entire time. Now he's throwing out puns like, "You're such a *boob*," just to stay in it, and rubbing his neck. He looks jarred not to hear applause from the weary crowd after each pun, a contrast to the amped-up Punderdome audience.

"Oh my God, I'm so sorry for this one," Jerry says, preemptively cringing at what he's about to say. "Why don't you just *SIDS* down?"

Half the crowd laughs nervously.

"I have a worse one," Isaac says, "and my ship is heading toward it because it's *abort* of call."

All the Punderdomers ferociously cheer Isaac for his quick comeback, before we realize how loudly we're cheering an abortion joke and pipe down.

When Isaac makes a pun that involves a stoned expecting mother carrying *high*, the MCs debate whether to accept it. They are unfamiliar with the expression "carrying high," which infuriates the women of Punderdome.

"You don't know because you're not a woman!" Ariel yells.

After Janani's round, our sexism sensors are all on over-drive. Ben Ziek has made a pun since then about RuPaul, and we all parsed and dissected each word before concluding that it was devoid of offense. Similarly, the judges eventually see the light about Isaac's pun and let it through. Less than a minute later, though, he gets his third strike, for reusing umbilical as a cue word. He raises his hands in the air, as if the strike is a mistake, but it isn't. Just like that, as goes the umbilical, so goes Isaac's last lifeline in the competition. He's out.

All the Domers automatically root for our fellow travelers. We're the Away team, after all. This loyalty is tested, however, in the next matchup, in which Jerzy has to take on Janani. We cheer every clever pun he makes on the topic of Hair, but we cheer just as hard when she claps back.

"I brought all my people with me," Jerzy says a few minutes in, gesturing toward us. "But unfortunately my *crew cut* themselves on something very sharp."

Janani sways from side to side for a moment.

"If I don't come up with a pun soon, I'll *wave* good-bye."

"*Perm*anently," Jerzy clarifies, without missing a beat. Janani starts swaying again.

She puts up a hell of a fight, coming at Jerzy with everything she has, and even forcing him into a couple of strikes. After several more minutes, though, she stumbles, making a pun on "turban," which doesn't fly with the MCs.

"We have a separate topic for hats and headwear," David says. "We'll give you a chance to fix it, though."

Janani gazes out into the middle distance and says, "If I make the *cut,* let's celebrate."

Steve points out that cut has already been used. Janani smiles hopefully and says *"Cutlets*?"

"That's not a haircut," he says, flipping over a third strike. "That's a piece of chicken."

It's over. Jerzy goes to shake Janani's hand and she hugs him, leading Sam to chant, "They should date! They should date!"

When Tim and Toby are up, they both handily defeat their second-round opponents. It's particularly satisfying to watch Toby take down the Brillo-headed guy who knocked out Ariel. As we head into the third round, only eight punsters remain. Three of them are Gwiazdowskis. I take a look at the scoreboard off to the side of the pavilion, which features brackets of all the matchups so far. It appears that pretty soon, Toby and Jerzy will be competing against each other.

Although I'm fired up to see who will win, I no longer exist in human form, but rather as a spirit locked inside a seashell echoing with puns. The crowd is hanging on by a thread, too. Everybody either needs a stretch, or they're trying to figure out whether they have enough space to lie on the ground, facedown like a skydiver, and whether that's appropriate. One small child wearing a polo shirt with a bow tie lies slumped over, off in his happy place, while his mom eats a chimichanga. Another woman is using a plump Dalmatian as a footstool. Not a single cell phone remains unchecked. But there is light at the end of the tunnel. Through the haze of beer, sun, and a pulverizing amount of puns, the war of words is wrapping up.

At first, it looks like Punster of the Year Andy Balinsky, who has shed his Shakespeare costume for more of a Little League dad look, is going to dispatch with Tim quickly. On the topic of Glassware, Tim narrowly avoids a strike, awkwardly bouncing around onstage in Converses with no socks, trying to come up with suitable puns. He stands his ground, though, and eventually triumphs, looking nearly as surprised at this unexpected victory as his opponent.

We're hoping for a similar turnaround when Jordan starts struggling on the topic of Wind against Jerry, defeater of Isaac, but after only a couple minutes, he is vanquished.

Soon enough, it's an American Civil War in the house of Gwiazdowski: Jerzy versus Toby. I had long thought it was possible we'd see two brothers from this family go against each other here—just not these two. The category is Furniture, and the pair cycle through the easy puns like "*Sofa* so good" in record time. I keep looking back at their parents, seated nearby on a flannel blanket, to see whether they're cheering for either brother in particular. Like most parents, though, if they have a favorite, they are keeping it to themselves.

"What it must have been like growing up in that house!" Gary says, speaking for all seven hundred people here.

After a few minutes, the puns start degenerating as the furniture warehouse is liquidated.

"If other kinds of barbecue can't satisfy you, *can ribs?*" Jerzy says, looking around expectantly. The crowd is stone silent. Finally, he explains; it's a pun on "cribs." Yikes. This is by far the least comprehensible pun I've ever heard Jerzy make. Truly, it's difficult to see any situation besides this one in which those words could be considered a pun. Toby seems stretched just as thin, though. He's about to hit a five-count, so he just goes for it.

"I live in Wisconsin and my brother lives in New York. I wish he was *armoire*," he says. Nobody knows what this means.

"Around more," he clarifies.

Jerzy is about to respond and then he stops and scrunches his eyebrows, like he just registered what Toby said. Then he crosses the scrimmage line to go hug his brother. From this sweet moment, though, things go goofily dark. Jerzy's eyes practically bug out when his brother says, "I can't afford flowers so I'll be sure to have a *fern at your* funeral."

"Next time I see your car in the parking lot, Toby, *I-key-ya*," he responds.

Ten minutes in, Toby is about to go down. He starts babbling on a four-count, clearly buying time, before he ends on "I like when people *stair* at me."

Brian and Gary thoughtfully debate whether stairs are considered furniture and eventually they give Toby a strike. He now has five seconds to make another pun, which he holds off on doing until the last possible second.

"After having twins last year, my wife wants me to *pull out*."

This line gets one of the loudest, longest laughs of the entire day. Jerzy reaches over and gives him a high five.

On his next turn, Toby asks, "Can't you let *booth* of us win?"

Jerzy steps up to respond, almost talks and then doesn't. The count is at three, four. A look comes over his eyes. He's got something. Of course, he's got something. I can't wait to hear what it is. When Jerzy speaks, though, he speaks very quietly.

"Congratulations," he says and steps back.

Toby's jaw drops, along with most of the audience's, and his arms fly in the air, a human Y. He is overjoyed. He and Jerzy melt into a hug as everybody in the crowd screams. The entire Brooklyn group is on our feet, stunned. Nobody saw this coming. I can't help wonder whether if that had been Ben Ziek up there instead of his brother, would Jerzy have forged on, digging deep and dredging up something? Maybe not. Maybe Toby outplayed him, fair and square.

It's now down to the final four: Ben Ziek, Jerry Yan, Toby, and Tim. During a brief respite before the next round, Gracie comes over and joins our group.

"What did you think about that 'carrying high' bullshit?" Ariel asks her.

"I was screaming from the judges' table!" she says.

"There should really be a female MC," Ariel responds.

Gracie admits what she told me the previous night, that Gary and David wanted her to MC this year but she opted out.

"It seems too nerve-racking, and I don't want to get booed," she says, and then she looks at Ariel, Ally, and Sam's disappointed faces. "But I guess the judges get booed a lot anyway, so yeah, I'll do it next year."

The women of Punderdome all break out into big, face-stretching smiles, and then we wait around for the final rounds.

As satisfying as I would've thought it would be to see Ziek rip apart Jerry Yan, it is not. The kid gets a nosebleed going into the round, little bulbs of tissue burrowing out of his nostril, and his condition does not improve over the following fifteen minutes of torture. The two start off rapid-fire riffing on the topic of Currency—"Let me be *franc* with you," the inevitable *doll hairs*—with Ziek immediately returning everything Jerry serves his way, and Jerry firing back as fast as he can.

"Gonna be *washing tons* of clothing after this," Jerry says, pointing at his bloody nose.

"You better find a *tub, man*," Ziek says, and the crowd erupts in awed cheers. I'm amazed at how fast he responded, and how perfectly the response fit. He must've had Harriet Tubman's new dollar in his back pocket, saving it for just the right moment. It feels significant, like the legendary Shot Heard 'Round the World from the 1951 Giants/Dodgers pennant race—only nobody will ever remember this, even for one second.

The further along this round gets, the more Jerry looks like the ghost of someone who died from food poisoning. His face is tomato red, and his arms are cradling his torso as though his insides have liquefied and he's about to start leaking. Despite all that, I'm still impressed with Jerry's ability to keep up with his opponent. Ziek seems impressed, too.

"*Euro* really good punster," he tells Jerry, and it's one of the sweetest, nerdiest things that's happened all day.

"I went up against Ziek in the third round once," Gracie tells Ally and me. "The category was Fabric, so I thought I had it in the bag, but he had worked at a clothing factory or something, and he was pulling out words I've never even heard of."

This is what Ziek does. He bleeds you dry. He keeps going and going until you are dead and incapable of returning fire. He's a diabolical pun cyborg; the friendliest, most gracious and upbeat pun cyborg the competitive word circuit has ever seen.

After he and Jerry run through alternative forms of currency like spice, salt, and bullion, Jerry tries to make a pun on iridium. The judges debate it for a moment, but don't allow it. Jerry has lasted longer than most, but he's out.

Ziek moves on to the finals, where he was perhaps always headed. All that's left to be determined is whether Tim or Toby will join him. As the pair makes their way up to the stage, almost everybody from Punderdome starts chanting Tim's name. Then we remember that Toby's parents are sitting right behind us—even though Papa G is currently snoozing—and we stop.

The topic is Temperature, and both competitors seem too drained to think of even vaguely scientific puns. Things are going not very well for either Tim or Toby, but slightly worse for Tim, who has a strike. Then, a few minutes in, Toby stumbles. He starts talking to buy himself time, laying tracks ahead while the train is moving, and what he settles on is that temperature, as a topic, is "very cool." The judges rule that this is not a pun, to which the audience revolts. The ruling stands anyway.

"*That's* not cool!" Ally yells.

Toby has five seconds to come up with another pun.

"I *heat* another second," he says, but "heat" has long since waved good-bye as an option. It's a second strike.

"Your brothers are good at punning, but I'd hate to see your *son burn* you at this," Tim says, a forecast about the next generation of Gwiazdowski punsters.

Toby has no comeback at first. He grimaces, his cheeks practically touching his eyebrows. You can see the gears spinning in his head, looking for purchase. Then he swipes his mic through the air like he's slamming a door. He's finished.

Tim has done it. There will be a Punderdomer in the finals of the 2016 O. Henry.

At some point leading up to his face-off with Andy Balinsky, Tim realized he was going further in this competition than he'd prepared for, and he stopped drinking whiskey and beer. Although the resulting partial sobriety has been the wind beneath his wings up until now, Tim looks unsteady on his feet as he gets ready to battle a ten-minutes-rested Ben Ziek. He realizes the topic is Periodic Tables, and you can almost see his spirit crush like a soda can. Then he waves his fists like he's reeling in fish while punching them, and shakes Ziek's hand.

If I were a betting man, I would never in a million years put my money on Tim. It only takes one minute for this investment strategy to prove sound.

"I wish I paid more attention in chemistry class . . ." Tim says, before bowing out.

Jerzy shakes his head and snorts. He knows his periodic tables better than the tables he couldn't quite conjure in the furniture round. If he were up there, he could take Ziek. Maybe.

It's an anticlimactic end to the competition. Ziek wins his

fifth Punslingers at the O. Henry, which likely won't be his last. He'll certainly have Tim, and Jerzy and one or two other Gwiazdowskis hot on his heels again next year, though.

"My first year, I came in second, too," Ziek tells Tim, as the two are shaking hands. "So you're set up to win next year."

"You guys are on so much of a higher level than we are," David Gugenheim tells the two of them, smiling through weary eyes. "Or 'were,' I guess."

HERE'S HOW MUCH the O. Henry crowd loves puns. After something like seven hours of puns in the arid Texas heat, thirty people show up to the after-party for more. It never stops, the churn of wordplay. Not here, not ever. It's a babbling brook whose whooshes howl through the forest until the end of time.

The party is at a family-friendly Mexican restaurant, with ambulatory, mustachioed jalapeños on the walls. Amid sizzling plumes of fajita steam, the MCs, organizers, contestants, and attendees line up to play pun games that inspired some of the ones Jerzy and Jordan play on their podcast. Ziek makes a pun and looks out at the crowd like a golfer tracking his ball to see where it lands. Newly crowned O. Henry MVP Janani Krishnan-Jha makes a pun and looks at her mother, who is clearly proud of this bright, talented young woman, who makes competitive punning seem less weird than it is. ("This is like the best day of my life," she tells me.) Isaac makes a pun and smiles to himself when he gets the big laugh. He didn't do as well as he wanted, but there's always Punderdome.

We don't stay for very long. Instead, we explore nocturnal

Austin. Ubiquitous bike racks, women in silver elastic space pants, vegan cheeseburgers at Cheer Up Charlies, unexplained Batman costumes on patio bars. Everybody is still high off our big showing at O. Henry, and we keep collecting people from the competition like Michael the Trump impersonator and a woman named Anika who went down in the first round of Punslingers. We go dancing at Hotel Vegas and Sam finds herself in a *Step Up*–style dance-off with a guy whose jean shirt is unbuttoned to the navel. We walk through the Pecan Street Festival, which at night turns into a Bourbon Street monstrosity, overflowing with boozed-out frat bros. Still, Isaac manages to get in a rap battle and holds his own better than anybody expects. Everyone is in his or her element, or they have multiple elements that all inform each other.

Toward the end of the night, someone raises the idea of getting a pun tattoo.

"All right, I'd be down," Tim says.

"What's a good pun tattoo?

"Don't get one!"

"That's not a pun."

"A pun is a thing that means another thing," I say, several sheets to the breeze and barely holding it together. "It's a cryptograph. So maybe like a Rosetta stone?"

"We can write 'ling' and it will be an '*ink*ling.'"

"Let's keep the brainstorm going!"

We talk about it for a little longer and then the topic disperses like a game of Movie Title puns. Probably for the best. The idea of a tattoo runs utterly counter to what we love about puns. The moment the right pun happens, and you were there to see the elements come together—that's what makes a pun,

not the Brundlefly of words. Puns are ephemeral, imperma-
nent, temporary visitors. Whatever was said is almost beside
the point—it's the situation itself, the people who were there,
the way that you laughed. And then it's gone. A tattoo could
never bring it back. You had to be there.

# CONCLUSION

The night we return from Austin, the Gwiazdowski brothers host their first live podcast at the People's Improv Theater in Manhattan. Most of the O. Henry crew show up to help give the games more variety, like the time we all recorded together in DUMBO so many months ago. The turnout is better than decent, and the laughs are steady. It's a markedly different format than Punderdome, the competitive aspect excised, but the crowd seems nearly as engaged as they do when the clap-o-meter is involved. It's a bold step toward the future of the podcast.

The episode never comes out.

A few weeks after recording, the brothers get into a heated argument and Jordan leaves the show. Jerzy promises he'll revive it someday, but for now *Punk Assed* is over. At the same time, Ariel and her pun partner, Tracy, are almost out of beta with their own pun podcast, which should be ready soon.

Later in the year, Jerzy gets a job at the New School teaching in the BFA drama program. He says he still wants to be a comedy writer for a late-night talk show some day, even though he hasn't tried stand-up at an open mic yet. Around the time he takes the teaching job, he also cuts his hair. He no longer looks like a magician.

Ben Ziek never got called back for *Jeopardy!,* but he plans on taking the online test again in October.

After the O. Henry, Tim is punned out and ready to take a sabbatical from the Dome. When Brokelyn hosts the official release party for the Punderdome card game, he lets Sam do the honors alone. A month later, Sam releases a video of fashion puns through *InStyle* magazine. It gets a ton of views, and she is excited to make more videos.

In June, Jonah Spear launches the first East Coast version of his Bay Area Pun-Off, the simply titled New York Pun-Off, in a loft in Manhattan. Not as many people show up as they did to the first event in San Francisco, but Jonah is enthusiastic. Meanwhile, in D.C., former Dome champ Brian Agler, a.k.a. Punda Express, has been helping a new competition called Beltway Pundits get off the ground. Later this year, he'll move back to New York and revive Punda Express.

Also over the summer, Toby Gwiazdowski graduates from competing in Pundamonium in Milwaukee, to hosting it.

At the Punderdome in July, I get my first-ever 10 from the clap-o-meter, on the topic of Amusement Parks. While waiting for my turn, I fixated on the words scattered across my board and they started to cohere into a story.

"I proposed to my girlfriend recently," I said. "And I was a little nervous, so I ducked into a *safety bar*. My stomach was growling but I ate a *ton-of-o-loves*. Then I got down on *dis-knee*, and said 'It's *you-n-I-vs. all.*' After that, I did a *ring toss*. And though she was wearing a chastity belt, she finally removed her *Bush guardin's*."

I delivered the monologue with a confused smile and a vocal uptick at the end of each sentence, like I was a little embarrassed but I absolutely had to share this weird true story. The funny thing is, it was the truth. Well, not entirely the truth. I'd long ago proposed to my wife, and it didn't go anything like that, but the presentation was truthful. I *was* a little embarrassed, and I *did* feel confident enough in my routine that I absolutely had to share it. I'd finally found a pun style: just being myself.

"Is that true?" Fred asked afterward.

"Sort of, but we definitely slept together before I proposed."

When the clap-o-meter rated my applause at a 10, I basked in the satisfaction of finally getting past the first round, after eight Punderdomes and one turn at O. Henry. The only problem was that three other people got 10s that round, a Dome record. It wasn't a lenient clap-o-meter either—the quality of the punning here just keeps improving, making it harder sometimes to distinguish a winner.

After three slapdash clap-offs, during which I quickly ran out of dance moves and ended up squat-thrusting, the other three 10s were chosen to move on to the next round. Nikolai, Ariel, Jerzy, and Jordan all congratulated me, though. They knew what this turn meant. Not that I was on their level yet—not even close, really—but maybe I was one of them after all.

In late July, Punderdome had its second annual battle against the *New York Post* team at the Highline Ballroom. It was almost exactly a year since the previous one, the first pun competition I'd ever seen. On the day of the event, Ally started a text thread, trying to coordinate a meetup. As always, the thread promptly degenerated into puns.

"A defeat for News Corp. will be good for what *Ailes* them," Ariel wrote.

"Don't *Hannity* victory to us just yet," Jerzy wrote.

"It didn't take *O'Reilly* long time for these puns to come out," I added.

The puns went on and on, but then Isaac mentioned that he wouldn't be able to make it that night. Neither could Ariel or Tim. And I didn't go either. It wasn't that I was done with puns, but it felt like less of a priority. Just as puns only last a moment, so do the roster of regulars at Punderdome. It comes in waves, like the shifting of the guard at O. Henry, or the funniest pun you can remember. Going to Punderdome every month forever is as impractical as a pun tattoo. I know I'll keep going, if for no other reason than to see what my friends will say—and what I will say—when we get onstage. I want to see the graffiti castle get scrubbed and redecorated again every month. But I've also got my popcorn ready for whatever they do outside of the Dome—whenever Jerzy writes his next play, or Rekha's pilot gets picked up, or anyone else makes something that lasts.

# ACKNOWLEDGMENTS

This book would not have been possible without the following people: Stephanie Hitchcock, my editor and the world's least likely @*midnight* superfan; Noah Ballard, my very handsome agent; Eric Alt, my very understanding editor at *Fast Company*; Jo Firestone, Fred Firestone, Tim Donnelly, Jerzy Gwiazdowski, Jordan Gwiazdowski, Rekha Shankar, Ally Spier, Melton Sharpe, Max Parke, Isaac Klein, Ariel Boone, Sam Corbin, Nikolai Vanyo, all the regulars at Punderdome, Alexandra Petri, Benjamin Ziek, Gary Hallock, David Gugenheim, Brian Oakley, Big Poppa E, Valerie Ward, Arthur Simone, Southpaw Jones, Matt Pollock, Dav Wallace, Dr. Richard Lederer, Dr. Vinod Goel, Dr. Christian Hempelmann, Dr. Salvatore Attardo, Peter McGraw, Neil Strauss, Shea Serrano, Joshua Foer, Elliott Kalan, Stuart Wellington, Dan McCoy, Wendy Molyneux, Lizzie Molyneux, Josh Gondelman, Jensen Karp, Myq Kaplan, Eliza Skinner, Zach Sherwin, Paul F. Tompkins, Jen Kirkman, Randy Sklar, Alex Blagg, Allie Goertz, Bob Mankoff, Brian Agler, Jonah Spier, Gracie Deegan, Diana Gruber, Deb Pines, Brayden Simms, Margi Conklin,

Darren Walsh, Ed Toutant, Greg Behrendt, Joe Randazzo, Emmy Blotnick, Kevin Porter, Jason Zinoman, Joe Sabia, Loren Bouchard, Mike Drucker, and Sean Gray. You are all champions in some way or another, whether you've won Punniest of Show or not.

# ABOUT THE AUTHOR

JOE BERKOWITZ IS an editor and staff writer at *Fast Company*, covering entertainment and pop culture, and he's also written for the *Awl, Cosmopolitan, Salon, Rolling Stone, Vulture, BuzzFeed, GQ,* and the *Village Voice*. He is the coauthor of *You Blew It: An Awkward Look at the Many Ways in Which You've Already Ruined Your Life.* He lives in Brooklyn with his wife and an ideal tuxedo cat.